MILTON'S LATIN POEMS

Milton's Latin Poems

TRANSLATED BY DAVID R. SLAVITT

Introduction by Gordon Teskey

The Johns Hopkins University Press
Baltimore

For Janet

© 2011 The Johns Hopkins University Press
All rights reserved. Published 2011
Printed in the United States of America on acid-free paper
9 8 7 6 5 4 3 2 1

The Johns Hopkins University Press
2715 North Charles Street
Baltimore, Maryland 21218-4363
www.press.jhu.edu

Milton, John, 1608–1674.
    [Poems. Selections]
    Milton's Latin poems / translated by David R. Slavitt ; introduction by
Gordon Teskey.
        p.   cm.
    ISBN-13: 978-1-4214-0078-5 (hardcover : alk. paper)
    ISBN-10: 1-4214-0078-2 (hardcover : alk. paper)
    ISBN-13: 978-1-4214-0079-2 (pbk. : alk. paper)
    ISBN-10: 1-4214-0079-0 (pbk. : alk. paper)
    1. Milton, John, 1608–1674—Translations into English. 2. Latin poetry,
Medieval and modern—England—Translations into English. I. Slavitt,
David R., 1935– II. Title
    PR3571. A2S63 2011
    871'.04—dc22   2010043037

A catalog record for this book is available from the British Library.

Special discounts are available for bulk purchases of this book.
For more information, please contact Special Sales at 410-516-6936 or
specialsales@press.jhu.edu.

The Johns Hopkins University Press uses environmentally friendly
book materials, including recycled text paper that is composed of at
least 30 percent post-consumer waste, whenever possible. All of our book
papers are acid-free, and our jackets and covers are printed on paper with
recycled content.

Contents

THE BOOK OF THE WOODS

INTRODUCTION

Gordon Teskey
Harvard University

In introducing David R. Slavitt's spirited translation of the Latin poems of John Milton (1608–1674), it may be helpful to state briefly, even for those who could answer the question themselves and at length, who Milton was, why he is important today, and how he became who he is. Milton is remembered as the second poet in English, after Shakespeare, for such masterpieces as "On the Morning of Christ's Nativity," "L'Allegro" and "Il Penseroso," *Comus* (as *A Mask Presented at Ludlow Castle* is popularly known), "Lycidas," and especially *Paradise Lost,* the classical epic on a Christian subject which Milton composed in his fifties, toward the end of his life. (The second, definitive edition would appear only months before his death.) He went on to write two more great works, *Paradise Regained* and *Samson Agonistes* (assuming, as is reasonable, the later date for this latter work), which critics regard as even more intensely focused on his central theme: human freedom under God and its relation to political action. But for elevation of mind and sublimity of form, *Paradise Lost* remains the work on which Milton's fame rests. On the highest peak of the English Parnassus, three works stand apart from and a little higher than the rest: William Shakespeare's *King Lear,* Herman Melville's *Moby-Dick,* and Milton's *Paradise Lost.*

When he composed *Paradise Lost,* Milton was totally blind, nearly destitute, in political exile, and for a time in danger of either legal execution or assassination in the London streets. What exactly did Milton achieve under such difficult conditions? The only fully successful and thoroughly classical epic poem written in the modern world, in a modern language, and on a theme altogether foreign to the values and outlook of the classical world. The theme is the Fall of Man and the prophetic vision of history arising from that fall. *Paradise Lost* achieves a difficult amalgam of the two great but very different and finally incompatible spiritual traditions in the imagination of the West: on the one hand, the brilliant and diverse literary productions of Greek and Roman classical antiquity; on the other hand, the single, coherent vision of history emerging from the Hebrew and Christian writings that make up the Bible.

Milton began working with the elements of this amalgam in his Latin poems, and in this respect he was a man of his time, the time of the revival of the art and literature of classical antiquity known as the Renaissance. Although he came late to this cultural movement, in the seventeenth century, when the foundations of modern science and liberal politics were already being laid (he had a deep interest in these, also), Milton was more successful than anyone before him at assimilating the glories of ancient literature to the purposes of a very different world. (A similar case could be made for Shakespeare's adaptation of Roman comedy, but Shakespeare's tragedies are too original to owe much to the comparatively thin tragedies of Seneca.) For this assimilation of classical forms into a Christian vision, Milton stands in the company of the greatest geniuses of the visual arts in the Renaissance, Raphael and Michelangelo, and as an artist, perhaps only Michelangelo stands shoulder to shoulder with him. Like those artists, Milton's achievement began in boyhood, in rigorous and minute training in the imitation of the art of the classical world—in his case Greek and Latin poetry, especially Latin poetry. He was taught to compose in a style as close as possible to that of the ancients, especially Virgil and Horace and still more especially his beloved Ovid, whose more informal couplets of uneven length, imitated here in the elegies, gave Milton his favorite Latin metrical form.

The Latin poems thus played a vital role in the technical development of Milton's English verse, leading to the final achievement of his grand style. But they are fascinating in their own right. Slavitt's own poetic gift captures the three principal characteristics of Milton's Latin poems which make them delightful in themselves as well as important for what is to come: their elegance, which would later mature into grandeur; their sly wit, which would later mature into insight; and their moral seriousness, which would later mature into hostility to tyranny—to what might be called *political sin*—because tyranny destroys human freedom.

Just as importantly, however, the Latin poems tell us much about who Milton was when he was young. The later prose works, which Milton wrote over some twenty years, beginning in his thirties, show him as a genius at the height of his powers, his learning lightly worn and lethally employed, aggressively engaged in the issues of the day. But even in their personal passages, when recollecting his youth, Milton's prose works are a less reliable witness than the Latin poems are to who the poet was on starting out. These poems are a fascinating record of the artistic and spiritual striving by which the young Milton began to take account of the range of his poetic gifts and to open to himself the depths of his own mind. What did he value? What did he think of himself and of his powers? How good was he? Was he merely promising, like a clever child, or did he have what it takes to be one of the great poets of the world, on a level with Homer and Virgil? How far could he go with his remarkable technical skill and his undeniably powerful ambition to surpass all others, in the present and especially in the past? Above all, what sort of work, what spiritual discipline, would best put him in the way to finding out? The answers to these questions are in the Latin poems, and the answer to the last—what discipline would set Milton on his way to finding out his greatness?—is the Latin poems themselves. They were Milton's singing school.

Just because the Latin poems were for him quite self-consciously a *school,* a training ground, they share with all school-like pursuits a gently mocking diffidence toward the high seriousness that they perform. Slavitt's translation brings out something the critics of Milton's Latin poems have generally missed: the irony that accompanies the playing of a difficult game, especially if one can afford a light touch because one is playing so exceptionally well. This irony may be absent from some of the more serious works, "Damon's Epitaph," for example, and at least the latter part of the epistle to Milton's old tutor, "To His Tutor, Thomas Young, Now Serving as Chaplain to the English Merchants at Hamburg" (Elegy IV), but for that very reason these poems are just a little duller than the rest. Their straightforwardness makes them heavy, taking away that power of flight, that soaring, which Milton so often associated with poetry. Milton is much more himself when he speaks, in the ode, "To John Rouse, Librarian of Oxford University," of writing years ago in a foreign country, and in a foreign language, while his feet were "not quite touching solid ground" (et humum vix tetigit pede). I might have rendered this more literally as, "his feet barely touching the ground," and so missed the sly modesty that is folded into the Latin phrase, which Slavitt captures with that *not quite*. The young poet whom Milton remembers from the safe distance of about eight years is so brilliant he is about to take flight, but he is also still an amateur and doesn't really know what he's doing.

This is only one small example of the subtle humor pervading Milton's Latin poems, even, perhaps especially, in the funeral elegies, since in the end their Christian purpose is to mock the gravity with which death is treated even by believers in the afterlife. The exception among the elegies, as I have mentioned, is "Damon's Epitaph," Milton's commemoration of his close boyhood friend, Charles Diodati, the only departed soul lamented in these poems about whom Milton cared. He feels sorry for himself but not for Charles, who even as his old friend Milton laments him is enjoying the eroticized honors of virgins married to the Lamb in the Heavenly Jerusalem ("while you reenact forever / the nuptial rites of immortals") and joining in what Milton calls, wildly juxtaposing the classical to the Christian, the raving Bacchic orgies under the thyrsus of Zion (Festa Sionaeo bacchantur et orgia thyrso). Of course, *orgia* (always in the plural) was a Greek word for secret, sacred rites. The association of the word with drunkenness and sexual license does not appear until its adoption into Latin. Perhaps, after all, Milton's irony is not absent even from this elegy for his friend.

When did Milton write his Latin poetry, and how did it fit in with his career as a poet in English? The early watershed of that career came shortly after Milton's twenty-first birthday, on Christmas morning 1629, when he composed his first undoubted masterpiece, "On the Morning of Christ's Nativity." Before that event, Milton had written comparatively little poetry in English: two psalm paraphrases, a translation of a short ode by Horace, and only four original works—a sonnet, a ten-line song, a hundred-line occasional poem in heroic couplets (in which, however, his high poetic ambitions are revealed), and a funeral elegy in the Spenserian manner, "On the Death of a Fair Infant Dying of a Cough." In contrast with this slender output in English, Milton wrote six poems in Italian, one poem in Greek, and fully nineteen poems in Latin, almost half of them of considerable length and one, "On the Fifth of November," a mini Latin epic of 211 lines, composed when Milton was only seventeen, in which, among other things, the devil takes an impressive flight down the Italian peninsula to persuade the pope to lay a plot to blow up the English parliament and King James. The years of study behind the massive geographical and cultural knowledge that saturates *Paradise Lost* are already bearing fruit:

> on pitch-black wings [Satan] soared through the air . . .
> He passed over the peaks of the snowy Alps and reached
> Italy [Ausoniae fines] where, on the left, the stormy Apennines lie,
> the land of the ancient Sabines, and opposite, on the right,
> Tuscany, notorious for sorcerers and magi [Dextra veneficiis infamis
> Hetruria].

After "Ode on the Morning of Christ's Nativity," however, the balance of his poems would shift to English.

Over the following eight years, up to the next decisive moment in his career, "Lycidas," written in 1637, Milton would compose only three Latin poems, although two of them are substantial (the sixth elegy and the poem to his father, of 90 and 120 lines respectively). This was Milton's breakout period in English, during which he would write twelve English poems (thirteen, if one counts "The Passion"), including the famous poem on Shakespeare; the immortal sonnet, "How soon hath time"; the elegant and touching "Epitaph on the Marchioness of Winchester"; the masterly pair of poems "L'Allegro" and "Il Penseroso," which are the most purely delightful works in Milton's entire canon; three less well-known but intensely beautiful poems on religious subjects; and finally, towering over the rest, *Comus*, or *A Mask Presented at Ludlow Castle*, which is over a thousand lines long. The *Mask* won wide public interest for its anonymous author and gave its first airing to the essential moral theme of *Paradise Lost*: that resisting temptation is freedom and giving into it bondage.

After "Lycidas," Milton would write seven more Latin poems, all but one of them within the next two years. ("To My Father," which is of uncertain date, may just follow or be approximately contemporary with "Lycidas.") The exception, written at age thirty-nine, in 1647, about a decade before he began *Paradise Lost,* is a technically virtuosic and facetious ode addressed to John Rouse, the librarian of the Bodleian library at Oxford, to accompany a copy of Milton's collected poems of 1645, a previous copy having been lost in transit. Of the Latin poems written after "On the Morning of Christ's Nativity," the sixth elegy, addressed to Milton's close friend, Charles Diodati, and especially "To My Father," contain serious reflection on the purposes of poetry and of humanistic learning. The two most ambitious Latin poems written after "Lycidas"—one, of one hundred lines, to the Italian marquis and famous literary patron, Giovanni Manso, who befriended Milton in Naples, the other, of 219 lines, a pastoral funeral elegy for Diodati—reflect seriously on the course to which Milton was now committed but deeply uncertain of his way: heroic poetry in English.

These poems do not, however, disappear into what Milton became. We do not read the Latin poems only to understand better the poet of

Paradise Lost; helpful as they certainly are in that respect, they can be misleading, too. The ethereal earthliness of the vision of the afterlife, in the elegy on the Bishop of Winchester (Lancelot Andrews), Elegy III, written around age seventeen, is astonishing in its own right, notwithstanding its being a premonition of the physical geography of the very earthlike heaven of *Paradise Lost*. There is delicate, almost self-mocking comedy in the lighter efforts, such as Elegy II, an efficient ululation of the long-lived University Beadle ("Cambridge now mourns for her lost friend . . . and let a dirge resound through all the schools"), who despite his swans-down hair is compared to the vigorous herald of the *Iliad*: "You stood like Eurybates, the royal herald, / When he confronted the wrathful Achilles, announcing the stern / command of Agamemnon, the Argive chieftan." A thick context of donnish irony and humor, now largely gone from our culture, underlies the poet's superficially daunting allusions, which are intended to seem slightly ridiculous, routinely comparing the small change of academic life with the heroic scenes of epic.

Awareness of the underlying facetiousness of tone goes some way to explaining, as I have said, the comparative dullness of Elegy IV, which Milton addressed to his former tutor, Thomas Young, who was in Germany at the time, a religious exile in danger from approaching armies and imminent war. Although most of it is intentionally absurd amplification on the topos of apology for not writing sooner, the elegy is undeniably impressive. Milton wants both to put on display the fruits of his teacher's care and to give thanks for showing him "the paths by which / [he] might ascend to reach the Pierian spring / and drink deeply." And so he does. But the relentless striving for seriousness in this poem sits ill with the usual forms of learned allusion as literary play. The personification of England "with a heart as hard as her famous white cliffs / where the waves beat on her shores" is close to the self-pity of puritan fanatics whose tribulations, as they called them, are only deflated by such comparisons as Milton now offers:

Even so was Elijah forced by Jezebel
  and Ahab to flee and tread the lonely paths
of desert wastes; thus was Paul of Tarsus, tortured
  and bleeding from the cruel lash, cast out
of Macedon; and thus did the Gadarenes send away
  Jesus from their city of ingrates.

Is it reasonable to compare a fugitive, choleric pedagogue with Elijah, Jesus, and Paul, or to liken his pigeon breast to the walls of Zion besieged by an Assyrian host with chariots and steeds? It is reasonable only if a joke is intended. Without facetiousness, the rich fruit of classical allusion withers on its overspreading vine. Total seriousness is all but impossible in this mode, and Milton usually exploits the fact. But it could be a problem when seriousness was really what he wanted. Milton had no solution until he wrote *Paradise Lost*, turning the problem inside out, so to speak, so that the material of learned allusion always ends up being smaller than what it is compared to.

As works of art, therefore, Milton's Latin poems are enjoyable and compelling in themselves just because of their droll exaggerations, even, as I have mentioned, in funerary moments, as when the departed university vice chancellor, Dr. John Gostlin, a physician, is told he would not have died if the queen of the underworld didn't resent him for the lives he saved in the exercise of his profession:

You would never have boarded Charon's skiff
to sail with him into the abyss.
  But Persephone was irked
  by the many cures you had worked.

The humor is especially evident in the best of the earlier Latin poems, Elegy V, "On the Approach of Spring," with its vision of the pagan gods, the sublime Olympians as well as the earthier satyrs and nymphs, in feverish tumult at the coming of spring. Earth bares her naked breasts to Phoebus, the sun-god, who is inflamed by her body, "touched with the delicate scents of Arabia's finest perfumes"; he is just as inflamed, touchingly, by the flowers in her hair. Our attention and pleasure, but also our respectful amusement, are commanded by those moments in the first and sixth elegies when Milton speaks so seriously of his higher poetic ambitions. But these are just as gloriously and absurdly on view when his intention is merely to celebrate the coming of spring:

> I feel my burning heart
> Beat in a tumultuous rapture I cannot ignore.
> Phoebus himself appears before me, his hair
> encircled by Daphne's laurel. My giddy mind is caught up
> in flights through the clouds and into the limpid heavens.
> My spirit is borne through the shades to the dwelling places of poets
> and the open shrines of the gods invite me to enter.
> My soul understands the enterprise of Olympian gods
> and sees into the secrets Tartarus holds.
> What splendor will issue forth to pour from my parted lips?

One is relieved to find Milton descends from such heights to speak of the pleasures of wine and song, though to the temperate bard the second was incomparably more important than the first. More pleasing still is his speaking of "Troops of maidens, their bodices belted in gold [going] forth / to the joys of the beautiful springtime" while we hear from the caves of the mountains the echoing invocations of the god of marriage—*Io, Hymen!*—who appears in splendid robes, "his tunic fragrant with crocus." As twilight falls and dolphins dance on the waves to the mariner's song, fauns and satyrs set off at a run in pursuit of tree goddesses and mountain nymphs.

Wonderful as the eroticized ancient landscape of Elegy V is, we are touched in Elegy I by Milton's loyalty, if that is the right word, to the "lovely virgins of Britain" (actually, of London), whose beauty is "like that of the stars, / or of jewels even brighter than stars, to revive the old age of Jove." The English girls are more beautiful than the beauties of old, now known only by their names, who were vaunted, courted, desired, and in the end very often reviled by the classical poets. For Milton, the intense lover of the classical world, it isn't easy to put yesterday's glories in their place, below the English girls, and doing so compels him to address to these snows of many yesteryears the following ungentlemanly command:

> Admit
>   you mistresses of myth who attracted the gods
> that these are at least your equals. Give precedence then you maidens
>   of Persia with your turret-high headdresses.
> You women of Susa and Memnon's splendid Nineveh, yield.
>   Even you famous beauties of Greece and Troy
> Must acknowledge these as your betters. Let the great Ovid hush
>   About his ladies of fashion who gathered together
> to see and be seen on Pompey's porch near the Roman theaters.
>   To these lovely virgins of Britain honor is due,
> while those of other times and nations must be content
>   to follow in their train.

The girls the young Milton sees while wandering the streets of London make the poet certain that the goddess of love herself, Venus, prefers Britain as her home to any of her Mediterranean haunts, such as her temples at Cnidos or on the island of Paphos, or in the valley of Simoïs' stream, where Paris fatally chose Venus as more beautiful than Minerva and Juno, setting in train events that would lead to the Trojan war— that is, to the super-serious world of the epic. Milton famously spoke of the rhetorical term *decorum,* the appropriateness of all elements of a discourse to the subject treated, as "the grand masterpiece to observe." But these poems rely for their subtle humor on the consistent and continual breaking of that rule.

On at least one occasion, in Elegy VII, the pleasure of watching girls goes beyond pleasure—though never, we may possibly regret, beyond restraint—when the poet is seriously wounded by Cupid's arrows, having been foolish enough to laugh at that powerful god. He is paralyzed with ardor by the briefest exchange of glances with a beautiful girl in the midst of a troop of only slightly less delicate beauties. To her, he suddenly gives his heart and soul. But in an instant she is snatched away from his sight, never to return. Even this sincere-seeming moment is not entirely straight-faced. It is instead poker-faced, as is what comes next in the edition of the poems Milton collected for publication in 1645: the supposition that even this brief glance of interest and desire between a boy and a girl exceeds the bounds of decency, at least for a sober, aspiring bard. Milton assures us he has packed his heart in ice and put aside erotic feelings for "the shades of Academe" and for the pleasure of walking beside "Socratic streams"—scenes not always so chaste as Milton supposed or, rather, as he pretended to suppose. For all his self-control, a powerful erotic current flows beneath the surface of Milton's poetry—and sometimes on its surface—from the beginning of his career to the end. It can be intoxicating and dangerous in *Paradise Lost*. In the Latin poems, it is meant to be at once genuinely affecting and funny.

The Latin poems also display, much more than Milton's English poems ever do (with the exception of "L'Allegro" and "Il Penseroso"), the intense pleasures of art, in which, for Milton, all other pleasures are fulfilled, or almost fulfilled. The pleasures of art include ancient theatre, mentioned in the first elegy (modern theatre is mentioned in "L'Allegro" and "Il Penseroso"), but otherwise literary art is to be enjoyed in solitude, where Milton is ravished by the beauty of the Greek and Latin poets, especially Ovid. Had he not been banished to the Black Sea by the emperor Augustus, Ovid would in Milton's opinion (as he says in the first elegy) have proved a greater poet even than Homer and Virgil—another facetious, semiserious claim. The funeral elegies are not only more ironical but also more exciting than their designation sounds, opening huge vistas on the universe and on the mysteries of the afterlife, as when, at the news of the death of the Bishop of Ely, the poet leaves his body and goes soaring into the heavens, beyond "the icy constellation of Boötes / and the terrible Scorpion's claws":

I flew beyond the gleaming orb
of the sun and I saw the moon below my feet,
as that golden triform goddess
checked her dragons tugging on golden reins.
Through the ranks of wandering stars
and through the Milky Way I was borne along
at a speed beyond comprehension
until I came to the shining gates atop Olympus.

The same thrills await the reader of the dry-sounding, philosophical poems, "That Nature Does Not Suffer from Old Age" and "The Platonic Idea as Understood by Aristotle," which show how closely Milton associates poetry with flight, with soaring to the ends of the earth and even to the poles of the cosmos. Such scenes are made more tremendous still when Milton imagines the apocalypse in "That Nature Does Not Suffer from Old Age." As king of the classical gods, Jove has the task of insuring that the heavenly bodies forming the mobile framework of the cosmos will "whirl in their proper orbits / forever." But one day,

the floor of heaven will tremble
and crumble and then, with a thunderous roar, all things shall fall
in ruins with the poles of the [universe] collapsing. Jove
shall tumble down from his celestial palace and with him
Athena too with her famous Gorgon shield uncovered . . .
   With their summits undermined,
The Balkans shall heave and tumble. The Ceraunian hills as well
That Pluto threw at the giants will fall to his Stygian realm.

This poem addresses a great theoretical debate of the day over what I suppose we would now call *entropy*, or its human manifestation, *pollution*. Is the natural world, it was asked, including the heavens, undergoing continual decay, as recent astronomical observation suggests, and as is brilliantly if perversely elaborated on by John Donne in his *Anatomy of the World*? The theme of the worsening of the world is a perennial favorite of doddering old men, such as the Earl of Gloucester in *King Lear,* with rosy views of their own youth. But is it true? Is the world getting worse, or is the order and health of the cosmos perfectly sustained by its Creator, at least until the end of time, at the apocalypse, when, as George Herbert says in a great poem, "all things burn." Milton splendidly imagines the apocalypse in this poem as all things collapsing. The question of the poem goes as far back as Edmund Spenser's great *Cantos of Mutabilitie,* published in 1609, the year after Milton was born. Milton piously argues for the position that the world is divinely sustained and does not grow old, but he can't resist saying—and he gets it done right at the start—that if there is any evidence of senescence in nature it is to be found in the erring minds of those who think it so.

"The Platonic Idea as Understood by Aristotle" is a gentle spoof on what seemed to Milton the excessive literalism of Aristotle's philosophy, or rather of Aristotelian philosophy by the successors to the Stagirite, including the Englishman William of Ockham, who said, "entities are not to be multiplied beyond necessity" (entia non sunt multiplicanda praeter necessitatem). My plate is real, and so is yours, but the idea of a plate, which allows us to use the same word for the two objects, is not real in the same way as the plates are, or perhaps in any way except as a name. (Hence, Ockham's followers were called *nominalists.*) To say the idea of the plate is real is to imagine an extra thing in order to explain similarity among things, as if an ideal bicycle were necessary to explain why bicycles are alike.

But Plato looks at this the other way round. He sees the plates themselves, and everything else around us in our world, as unnecessary, quasientities. Plato said all things are imitations of their ideal forms, which are more real and true than the actual things are. Of these ideal forms, the most important would seem to be the form of man. (Plato actually thought the most important was the form of the good, but subsequent commentary focused on the definition of man, and the most famous criticism of his philosophy was known as the "Third Man," an infinite regression which opens when a third man is imagined as mediating between the ideal man and particular men.) If the forms are more true than the things that derive their being from them, the forms must also be particular and solid beings, not just general names for categories, and they must have definite locations in space, either here or there. So the form of man must be a single being that actually exists and is more real than its imitations, more real than the swarm of individual men, such as you and me. (I use *men* for both sexes and retain the term because in all such discussions in the past the male was intended as the norm.)

Plato's philosophy was most congenial to Milton's idealism, and the young poet with his ardent moral convictions would hardly have resisted the call to imagine the perfect form of man, to which all others are imperfect approximations. One occasionally suspects, as in the closing lines of "Manso," that Milton has himself in mind for the role of perfect form of man. But by an ideal man he really means a moral ideal, a composite of perfect faculties and virtues which would be a metaphysical unity, a model or *paradeigma,* to use one of Plato's terms, not a material being locatable in space. Anyhow, Milton would later imagine just such a man as a material being, a morally and intellectually perfect human, locatable in space, from whom all other men and women derive. He is Adam, in *Paradise Lost.*

But many years before that invention, in "The Platonic Idea as Understood by Aristotle," Milton ventriloquizes Aristotle mocking the absurd consequences of Plato's idealism precisely by imagining those consequences embodied. The form or idea of man as "an individual unto himself in a portion of space" would have to be *somewhere,* on the far side of the moon, perhaps, or striding like a giant in some as yet undiscovered country on this earth, larger than Atlas, a huge, giant archetype of man (ingens archetypus hominis gigas) and frightening even the gods. Yet none of the great prophets of Greece, Assyria, and Egypt, "Aristotle" continues, wise as they were in the secrets of the world, had any inkling of such a man. What a wonderful thing! What a portent! Surely, you will remember, my revered teacher Plato, Milton's "Aristotle" concludes, with what is supposed to be the final knockdown, how you banished the poets from your ideal Republic because they invented fictional beings. But you are the greatest fabulist of all and will have to join the poets in exile.

The literalizing "Aristotle" is generally the target of the humor in this philosophical poem, which is a backhanded defense of Plato, although Milton can't help letting Aristotle strike a few fine blows. Plato's theory of the forms does not emerge entirely untouched by Milton's irony. Perhaps Plato really is something of a poet after all, which for Milton wouldn't be such a bad thing.

We are especially engaged by these poems for what they show us of Milton's poetic ambitions and hopes, as when, in Elegy I, he celebrates what would prove to be a very brief exile from the University of Cambridge, which he says is "not a proper place / for those of us who follow the great Phoebus / and set for ourselves the edifying task of producing poetry." One is not surprised and not entirely displeased to hear Milton was a discipline problem. Of special importance in this respect is Elegy VI, in which, after vigorously promoting the idea that the poet must enjoy the pleasures of life, especially wine and food ("Often up in the hills have the nine Muses exclaimed / *Evoë* and mixed in with the Bacchanalian revels"), Milton turns, with one of his telltale "buts," to another kind of poetry and another kind of poet, one whose ambition "is to sing grave songs of wars / and try to recount the workings of Jove in the world." Such a poet "must live a spare and abstemious life / as Pythagoras did . . . his drink must be pure water / in a wooden bowl fresh from a bubbling spring," and he must be "always chaste and free from the taint of sin." Such a poet "is sacred to gods and serves as a priest / for his heart and lips express the thoughts of an indwelling Jove."

Milton then goes on, in a startling moment, to tell his interlocutor, his close friend Charles Diodati, of an English poem he is working on and has actually completed. This is something Milton does not do elsewhere in the Latin poems, although he does speak later, in "Damon's Epitaph" and "Manso," of possible subjects from English history for the epic poem he aspires to compose. But here he refers to the recent, brilliant achievement of "On the Morning of Christ's Nativity" (it is not named by its title in the original Latin, but is unmistakably meant), which tells "of the great star and the hymns of the heavenly angels / and of Greek and Roman gods undone in their shrines." It was a vision given to Milton at the first light of dawn on Christmas morning and written down "in the strains of my native tongue."

The ability to write a poem of such cosmic and historical sweep, its passionate feeling expressed with perfect refinement, depended, of course, on genius, but it also depended on the poet's having had from his devoted, if exasperated, father the very best education money could buy. Milton attended an elite school, Saint Paul's, arguably the best in England at the time, and in Europe; tutors instructed him in what was not taught at school, sciences and modern languages; and there was no doubt a servant to keep the candles lit and in trim as the boy studied late into the night. After taking two degrees at Cambridge, Milton did not go out to work, nor did he go into training in one of the professions, such as law. Instead, he continued to study at his father's house in the country, making the by no means easy transition from a brilliant student to a serious scholar. He did so, however, not in preparation for entering the church, objecting as he did to the hierarchy of Anglican bishops, but rather to prepare for the most demanding and unlucrative of professions, that of the poet.

Sometime, probably in his late twenties, Milton wrote a fascinating poem of handsome thanks and of subtler pleading to his father—thanks for the magnificent and expensive education he'd received (neither magnificence nor expense is left out of account), and pleading with his father not to scorn the muses or condemn the path Milton had chosen in life. Despite the poem's delicate and complex human purpose, for which one might have thought prose a better instrument (one would be mistaken in this instance), "To My Father" is a brilliant and not unhumorous display of the fruits of the poet's education, in which he proudly declares that all his possessions are displayed right there on the page, in the very ability to write such a poem.

However the poem was received, Milton's father continued to pay, and not long after we find Milton at age twenty-nine heading off, with a manservant, on a long journey to France and in particular to Italy, the home of the Renaissance. Milton traveled down the Italian peninsula, making friends among learned men, especially in Florence and Rome, and arriving at length in Naples, from whence after a stay his plan was to continue south into Magna Graecia and Sicily and perhaps by ship to Greece, the origin of the classical tradition. The outbreak of the English revolution turned him back from Naples, however, but not before receiving the spontaneous hospitality and friendship of an older, famous man, Giovanni Manso. To Milton, Manso was venerable for his having been the patron of and genuinely cared for the major Italian poet, Giambattista Marino, the founder of a wildly popular "school" of poets named after him, and also for the great Torquato Tasso, the only classical epic poet of the modern age before Milton, author of *Jerusalem Delivered* (as it is called in the great translation of Edward Fairfax, which Milton seems to have read for its excellent style, despite his own sufficiency in Italian). The fine poem to Manso is an inflated thank-you letter, but the praise of Manso's generosity to poets goes beyond mere thanks to celebrate a shared vision of the joyfulness of a life devoted to the muses: "Fortunate old man!" Milton says, "Fortunate senex!" cleverly echoing Virgil's congratulation, in the *Eclogues,* of a young man who is free enough, and rich enough—"fortunate puer!"—to meditate at leisure the pastoral muse.

Enough, if not much, has been said here, perhaps, of Milton's second-to-last Latin poem, "Damon's Epitaph," which concludes in heavenly orgies, and on his last Latin poem, the ode to the Oxford librarian who had requested a replacement for the lost copy of Milton's *Poems* of 1645. That book was in fact two books separately paginated with two title pages bound up into one, the English poems first and the Latin poems after: "Twofold book, got up in single dress / and yet with double pages . . . some that the author wrote in Ausonian shades, / and also some in the pleasant British landscape." (*A Mask Presented at Ludlow*

Castle, better known as *Comus,* was inserted, with its own title page and front matter, between the English and Latin poems but is continuously paginated with the former.) The poems written in "Ausonian shades" are the ones translated here—with the exception, of course, of this poem, which was sent with the replacement copy. The book and the ode that came with it are still in the library today, bearing out Milton's confidence that it would be read down the centuries to come.

I have said nothing on Milton's epigrams extolling the celestial beauty of the voice of Leonora Baroni, singing at Rome, though they illustrate a frequent theme of his, that music is not so much an expressive art as it is a way of harmonizing one's soul with the cosmos, a Pythagorean and Platonic theme adopted in the Christian Middle Ages. I have neglected the epigrams on the gunpowder plot, though I like them. Nor have I spoken of the metrically difficult and pleasing but otherwise unimportant verses addressed to the ailing Roman poet Salzilli, wishing him better health in a meter that imitates limping, which was a nice thing to do.

I conclude instead by returning to the conclusion of "Manso," which I briefly referred to before, where Milton imagines an altogether higher level and kind of immortality than what he was assured of by the presence, thanks to John Rouse, of that slender volume in the Bodleian library.

Manso had cared for both Marino and Tasso, who were impoverished at the end of their lives, an act of kindness that puts Manso in a class with Gallus and Maecenas, the great patrons of the Roman poets Milton so loved. Anticipating his own poverty because he is committed to poetry, Milton hopes a dear friend like Manso will likewise be there at the end of his life, take care of him on his deathbed, and gather his ashes into a simple clay urn.

But that isn't immortality or fame: it is caring. Milton therefore goes on to hope this friend will raise over his grave a marble bust of his features, wreathed with a poet's garland of myrtle and laurel leaves, beautifully carved in the stone: "my stone locks decked with a garland also of stone / but representing in marble branches of Cyprian myrtle / and the laurel boughs of Parnassus. I should then rest easy." But he is not easy, yet:

> If righteousness is rewarded in the way it deserves,
> I, removed to the high ethereal realm of the gods . . .
> shall look down and see these deeds of yours . . .
> and, with my mind serene, my face wreathed in smiles,
> and suffused with light, I shall clap my hands in thanks and praise.

The poet is at last in heaven, and it is a heaven for poets, Olympus (so it is named in the original Latin), the ethereal realm of the gods, where his mind is at last serenely at rest and his smiling face suffused with the purple light of the dawn, applauding his own funeral rites. But he is also in the eternity of the Christian heaven, where he may look down on all events in time, including his own deeds and the struggle of their accomplishment, with the tense anticipation one feels in the theatre. As we have seen him say before, "What splendor will issue forth to pour from my parted lips?" (Quid tam grande sonat distento spiritus ore?) He may also applaud Manso, the friend of poets, and a few others like him. But at this moment Milton allows himself to imagine his having reached that sublime coign of vantage to which all the restless soaring in his other verse strives. From that point alone may he applaud his epic art and life: "et simul aethereo plaudam mihi laetus Olympo" (while joyfully I applaud myself from ethereal Olympus). Shall we join him?

On the Titles and Ordering of Poems in This Volume

The English titles given in this volume follow the Latin titles Milton gave the poems when he published them in 1645, in *Poems of Mr. John Milton,* and when he republished them in 1673, in *Poems, & c. Upon Several Occasions. By Mr. John Milton.* (Milton's occasional practice of putting his age in the title, not always accurately, has been omitted here.)

In 1673 Milton added only two, formerly unpublished poems: "Fable of the Peasant and the Landlord" (1624) and "To John Rouse, Librarian of Oxford University." The latter, a noble and metrically challenging ode, was composed in 1647, two years after the 1645 *Poems*. Its occasion was the loss in transit of a copy of the 1645 *Poems,* intended for Oxford's Bodleian library. Milton sent the manuscript of the poem (though the manuscript is not in his hand) with a replacement volume. Both remain in the Bodleian today. "Fable of the Peasant and the Landlord" is most likely a school exercise, though it is pointedly wise, and it is in elegiac couplets, a meter most congenial to Milton.

One sees why Milton declined to include two other school exercises, which were not discovered until the nineteenth century and are also not included here. In Milton's day, boys were required to rise exceptionally early for school and to endure a very long school day. Both poems, on what was probably an assigned topic, come out firmly against oversleeping: "Carmina Elegiaca" (Elegiac Verses), which begins, "Surge, age, surge . . ." "Wake up! Come on! Wake up!"; and the untitled poem scholars learnedly refer to as "Verses in Lesser Asclepiads," or "Ignavus satrapam . . . inclytum" (It is Ignoble for a Famous Prince). What is ignoble for a famous prince to do? To lie out flat in his purple, or luxurious bed—"stratus purpureo procubuit toro"—lest his army be attacked in the night.

The Lesser Asclepiad is a line is built around two thumping, choriambic feet, preceded by two free syllables (i.e., they can be long or short) and followed by an iamb. Allowing for an approximation of English stress verse to Latin quantitative verse, an English Lesser Asclepiad would have the following rhythm: "Oh my, what a mistake! Now I'll be late! Okay?" For a sixteen year old to write even eight lines of this rhythm in Latin and make any sense at all is an accomplishment, but one the author of *Paradise Lost,* at age sixty-five, no longer felt it needful to disclose.

How did Milton organize his Latin poems, to what extent is his organization followed in David Slavitt's volume, and to what extent is it changed? The basis of Milton's ordering is the 1645 volume, in which the Latin poems, called *Poemata,* appear at the end, with a separate title page and separate pagination, as noted above. The poems are distributed in two parts, or "books": *Elegiarum liber,* "The Book of Elegies" and *Sylvarum Liber,* "The Book of the Woods." Both titles refer to the meter of the poems in them, not to genre or subject matter. The *Elegiarum liber* contains poems written in Latin elegiac couplets, where *elegiac* refers exclusively to the meter and has nothing to do with the genre of the funeral elegy. There are in fact two funeral elegies in this book, but there are three more in the *Sylvarum liber,* including Milton's greatest Latin funeral elegy, "Epitaphium Damonis." One might reasonably expect something called "The Book of the Woods" to contain woods, but one would be wrong in this instance. The Latin word for a wood, *silva,* or its plural, *silvae,* was used for any volume of poems in various meters. When Milton in 1673 added "Fable of the Peasant and the Landlord" and "To John Rouse, Librarian of Oxford University," he put the first in the *Elegiarum liber* because it is in elegiac meter and the second in *Sylvarum liber* because it is not. (It is in fact a complex experiment in various Greek and Latin meters.) There is no deeper reason for this distribution of the two poems. In sum, the unifying principle among the poems in *Sylvarum liber* is diversity of meters, and the unifying principle in *Elegiarum liber* is uniformity of meter.

In his arrangement of the poems for this translation, David Slavitt has adjusted a little in the direction of genre, a sensible decision when meter is usually imperceptible in translation. "The Book of Elegies" contains, in the order Milton numbered them, the seven poems actually called "elegies," plus the Retraction (as Stella P. Revard accurately calls it)—also in elegiac meter—which Milton put at the end of the series, although what is thus retracted is mostly the very mildly erotic subject matter of the seventh elegy. The untitled Retraction is separated from the seventh elegy—or from all the preceding elegies—merely by a solid line. The seventh elegy actually was written earlier than the fifth elegy and the sixth. It was moved into the later position because its subject matter makes a better prelude to the Retraction than does the discussion of poetry in the sixth elegy.

The eight epigrams, also in elegiac meter, which Milton put after the seven elegies and the Retraction, are in the present volume put in a separate category: "The Epigrams." Two of Milton's epigrams have been dropped in the present volume—the third gunpowder epigram and the third Leonora Baroni epigram—and two more brought in from elsewhere. These are "Fable of the Peasant and the Landlord," the school-age poem that was published in 1673, and "On Salmasius," which appeared in 1653, when Milton was in his mid-forties, in the course of his second polemical attack in Latin prose on the European scholar, Claudius Salmasius, who had been hired to write against the English Revolution and the execution of Charles I. In the poem, Milton mocks Salmasius' worthless writing, saying its pages will be used to wrap fish and wipe noses. An earlier Salmasius epigram ridiculing a technical blunder in his grammar appeared in similar circumstances in 1650. Milton published neither of these Salmasius poems in 1673, and the translator has passed over the less amusing, earlier one.

For further textual information on Milton's Latin poems, see the two indispensable editions, John Carey, *John Milton: Complete Shorter Poems,* 2nd ed. revised (Edinburgh Gate, Harlow, UK: Pearson/Longman, 2007), which is chronologically arranged; and Stella P. Revard, ed., *John Milton: Complete Shorter Poems and Latin Poems,* trans. Lawrence Revard, (Malden, MA; Chichester, UK: Wiley-Blackwell, 2009), which is arranged by publication.

Chronology

Dates are often approximate. (* = poems not included in this volume)

The Book
of Elegies

The First Elegy
To Charles Diodati

At last, dear friend, your letter has reached me here with words
    from the western bank of Chester's River Dee
the swift waters of which flow down to the Irish Sea.
    It is indeed a comfort to me to think
how at such a distance there can be so loving a heart
    and a head so full of wisdom. I look to the day
when that remote milieu that holds my pleasant companion
    will oblige me by returning him to me.
I am now in the city washed by the ebbing and flowing Thames
    where it is pleasant to while away my time   10
beneath my father's roof. To return to the reedy Cam
    is not my present desire: its barren fields
that lack any gentle shade are not a proper place
    for those of us who follow the great Phoebus
and set for ourselves the edifying task of producing
    poetry. The reproofs of a harsh tutor
and the threats, not always empty, are hardly what I require,
    and to these my proud nature will not submit.
If this rustication of mine is supposed to be an exile,
    the punishment is this carefree leisure and ease.   20
If no worse blow had fallen upon the poet of sadness
    who wrote the *Tristia* out at the end of the world,
he could have been the equal of the great Ionian Homer,
    and Virgil would not have been Rome's greatest poet.
Here I may spend my time with the tranquil Muses and books
    that are my life and absorb me altogether.
When I weary of these and need a change, I have the theater
    to call me from my study and offer diversion—
the grasping old man enraged by the spendthrift heir,
    or the lover or the sly off-duty soldier,   30

or the lawyer who has grown rich on a case that has gone on
    for ten years while he babbles in wretched Latin
to a court that apparently knows even less than he does,
    or the sly servant who helps the love-stricken son
avoid and evade the stern but all too gullible father.
    And then there's the innocent maiden, wide-eyed with wonder
at the first pangs of a love that has taken her unawares.
    Tragedy rages, waves her gory scepter,
and rolls her eyes in passion and shakes her disheveled locks.
    I look upon her in a pain that is also pleasure,   40
where sweet and bitter tears are artfully mixed together:
    an unhappy youth dies who has never tasted
the joys of love and he perishes lonely and unlamented;
    or the cruel avenger crosses the Styx to appear
with her baleful torch that she waves to remind us all of our sins.
    Or I watch the stories unfold of the house of Thyestes
or I follow the sad business of proud Troy's downfall,
    or the story of Oedipus and then of Creon.
But not all of my pleasures are indoors. Even here
    in the city spring comes bringing delight   50
to those who look about them. I visit the thick elm groves,
    and I wander in contemplation in their shade.
At times I encounter bands of young attractive girls
    and pause to admire their beauty, like that of the stars,
or of jewels even brighter than stars, to revive the old age of Jove.
    Their willowy necks, their light-brown wind-blown hair,
their alluring cheeks that rival the anemone's red that sprang
    from the blood of Adonis . . . these are the golden snares
set out for men by the wily god of Love. Admit
    you mistresses of myth who attracted the gods   60
that these are at least your equals. Give precedence then you maidens
    of Persia with your turret-high headdresses.

You women of Susa and Memnon's splendid Nineveh, yield.
   Even you famous beauties of Greece and Troy
must acknowledge these as your betters. Let the great Ovid hush
   about his ladies of fashion who gathered together
to see and be seen on Pompey's porch near the Roman theaters.
   To these lovely virgins of Britain honor is due,
while those of other times and nations must be content
   to follow in their train. Here in turreted London,   70
the city built by pious Aeneas' grandson Brutus
   and famous throughout the world, how happy we are
to have within our walls so great a share of the beauty
   of which out planet can boast. As many stars
as shine in the sky in the train of the moon, Endymion's goddess,
   so many lovely girls and women do we have here.
It was to this island that Venus, borne by her team of doves
   and followed by her loyal train of archers,
came to dwell preferring this to her temple at Cnidos
   or that of Paphos, and even the Simoïs' valley   80
where Paris selected her as the most divinely lovely.
   It will take some determination to turn away
for such temptations as those the blind boy has on offer,
   but with the moly to guide my feet along the path
as it did in the infamous palace on faithless Circe's island,
   I shall return to the Cam and once more endure
the hoarse murmur of schools. But for now, accept
   this tribute of words of unequal measures.

The Second Elegy *At the Age of Seventeen*
On the Death of the Cambridge University Beadle

With your shining staff of office you summoned the fellows together,
    but now in a dismal reversal of roles Death,
the world's ultimate beadle, has summoned you
    nor has he shown any favor to his colleague.
The hair on your temples had turned as white as the swan feathers
    Jove put on to disguise himself for Leda.
You would have been worthy to drink Medea's potion
    with which she restored Aeson to strength and youth.
Aesclepius, it is said, restored the dead and brought them
    back from across the dark waves of the Styx.   10
Would that he could perform the same astonishing service
    and recall you, too, to life and the light of the sun.
When you were exercising your official powers here,
    you were like Hermes, the messenger of the gods,
whom Zeus sent to speak in the palace halls at Troy.
    You stood like Eurybates, the royal herald,
when he confronted the wrathful Achilles, announcing the stern
    command of Agamemnon, the Argive chieftain.
O Death, Avernus' intransigent attendant,
    why can you not find it in yourself   20
to spare those who follow the nine Muses and those
    who are Athena's acolytes and servants?
Why not pick from among lesser, less useful men
    and aim your fatal arrows into the crowd?
In our sable robes, Cambridge now mourns for her lost friend.
    Let his bier be wet with all our tears.
Let Elegy pour forth in her sad and unequal measures
    and let a dirge resound through all the schools.

The Third Elegy   *At the Age of Seventeen*
On the Death of the Bishop of Winchester

In solitary silence I sat with a burden of griefs
  that weighed upon my soul when there appeared
the phantom of the plague that Libitina had sent,
  that ancient Roman goddess of corpses reaching
here to England. Grim Death with her smoky torch
  entered the marble palaces of great men,
smiting the stately walls that were rich in jasper and gold
  and made bold to swing her sharp scythe
and in a frenzy mow down troops of our great nobles.
  I call to mind Christian, Duke of Brunswick,   10
and his brother-in-arms Ernest, Count of Mansfield, their bones
  consumed in the smoke of their untimely pyres.
I remember Sir Henry Vere, the Belgian hero, caught up
  in heaven's clutches and leaving his friends to mourn.
But chiefly I am thinking of you, most noble Bishop
  who once was the crowning glory of Winchester.
I dissolved into tears and in the depths of grief complained:
  "Cruel Death, you goddess next in power
to Jove himself, how can you not be satisfied
  that forests suffer your anger? The grass of the fields,   20
the lily, the crocus, the rose sacred to Venus wilt
  at the touch of your maleficent exhalations.
You do not even permit the mighty oak that stands
  beside the flowing river to gaze forever
at its running water. From birds, those harbingers of the future,
  borne as they are on wings through heaven's liquid,
you collect their debt, as you do from the thousands of beasts
  that wander the woods or lurk in Proteus' caves.
They all succumb to you. As powerful as you are,
  what joy can there be for you to stain your hands   30

in the blood of humans and drive your unerring shafts
    into so noble a breast and drive out a soul
more than half-divine that made its home therein?"
    It was thus that I considered these grave matters,
until the rising of Hesperus out of the sea while Phoebus,
    completing his round, submerged his shining car
into the welcoming waves. I laid myself down on my bed
    in the hope that I might find some peace and repose.
In not very long my eyes had closed and sleep possessed me—
    and then it seemed that I wandered in some field,   40
but I have no gift that would let me describe what I saw there.
    The light was rich and strange and all things glowed
in a purple tinge, as when, in the morning, mountain peaks
    redden in the rising sun's first light.
Thus must it have been when Iris scattered her dazzling
    colors throughout the world. Zephyr's Chloris
could not have adorned Alcinoüs' splendid garden with more
    or any greater variety of flowers.
Silver streams wound through the verdant meadows with sands
    a richer gold than you'd find on the banks of the Tagus.   50
A gentle westerly wind tousled the fragrant leaves
    and dispersed the sweet scent of countless roses.
It is said at the Sun god's palace far off on the wide Ganges
    he maintains for his pleasure a similar garden.
I gazed in total wonder at all the sunlit spaces
    as well as at the shadows beneath the vines
heavy with grapes . . . And there, the Bishop of Winchester stood,
    his face lit with the radiance of stars.
He wore a long white gown that swept to his golden sandals
    and a wreath of white flowers adorned his head.   60
He advanced toward me and I felt the earth tremble with joy.
    Angels clapped their jeweled wings together

and the rich triumphal sound of a horn filled the air.
    That heavenly host saluted the Bishop and sang,
while one of them spoke in words that I could comprehend:
    "Come, my son, to your Father's joy and gladness
and delight in his kingdom in freedom forevermore from labor."
    At this, his companions touched their golden harps.
But my vision of peace ended with the coming on of Dawn
    and I wept for the loss of the dream I pray may return.   70

The Fourth Elegy   *At the Age of Eighteen*
To His Tutor, Thomas Young, Now Serving as Chaplain
to the English Merchants at Hamburg

Go, my letter, hurry across the boundless sea
    and seek across the blue expanse of the deep
the land of the Teutons. Do not dawdle along the way.
    Let nothing impede your progress. Make all haste.
I shall pray to Aeolus for favorable winds,
    and to Doris and her company of nymphs
to give you a smooth, peaceful, and expeditious crossing.
    If you can, why not try to get that speedy
team Medea used when she fled from her husband Jason?
    Or take the dragon car Triptolemus rode   10
when he carried Demeter's generous message and told the world
    how to sow and harvest crops in the field.
When you can see the yellow sands of the German shore,
    turn your course toward the walls of the port of Hamburg,
the name of which they say comes from Hama the Saxon
    killed on the spot where the city now stands
by a powerful Danish giant wielding a huge club.
    A pastor lives there, a simple and pious man,
who devotes himself to the care and feeding of Jesus' flock.
    This man is half my soul, and our separation   20
diminishes me, for I am forced to live without him.
    How many wide seas and lofty mountains
are standing between me and my other and dearer self!
    What Socrates, the wisest of all the Greeks,
was to pupil Alcibiades, he is even more
    to me. He means much more than the Stagirite
Aristotle did to his noble, promising pupil,
    Alexander the great, who was son of Jove.

What Phoenix the son of Amyntor, and Chiron, the centaur,
  were to Peleus' son, he is to me.   30
He was my guide when I took my first tentative steps
  onto the gentle but sacred lower slopes
of Helicon; he first showed me the paths by which
  I might ascend to reach the Pierian spring
and drink deeply. With Clio's permission I also imbibed
  from the sweet Castalian waters of Phoebus Apollo
in the hope that it might foster the talents of which he approves.
  Three times have Helios' horses in their rounds
passed through the sign of the Ram; twice has lovely Chloris
  bestrewn the earth with tender shoots and flowers;   40
and twice has Auster swept her lavish gifts away
  since my eyes were allowed to gaze upon his face
or my ears could delight in the sweet harmonies of his speech.
  Go then, and outdo the speed of the roaring winds.
Whatever difficulties you meet, you shall overcome,
  improvising and learning as you progress.
You will find him more likely than not beside his charming wife
  and fondling on his knee one of their children.
Or it may well be that he will be turning the folio pages
  of a learned text by one the ancient Fathers   50
or even the holy Scriptures, the words of the one true God.
  Or, no, I see him engaged in his good works
of shedding the dew of heaven on the souls of those in need
  of spiritual aid or physical healing,
these being the proper roles of men of faith.
  However you find him occupied, you must greet him
in a way that would be fitting for me, if I were there.
  Modestly, stare at the ground for a moment or two
and then address him, speaking these words on my behalf:
  "If in the midst of your strenuous undertakings   60

you have a moment of leisure to give to the gentle Muses,
    a faithful hand remits these verses to you
from England's shores. Tardy though it may be, accept
    this cordial greeting that may be all the more welcome
for its belatedness. Think how Penelope felt
    after those long years of waiting in hope
when the husband for whom she had yearned at last appeared before
        her.
    But why should I try to contrive these lame mitigations
for a fault so grave that he could not himself excuse it?
    He is charged and he pleads guilty to tardiness.   70
He confesses and he is ashamed of himself for failing
    in what was a clear duty. He asks forgiveness.
But sins that one confesses are already half-atoned,
    and he throws himself upon your generous mercy.
Sometimes the savage beast with its gaping jaws relents
    and does not tear out the life of its trembling prey.
The lion with its dreadful claws may spare its victim.
    Even Thracian spearmen have held their hands
at the fervent appeals of a suppliant kneeling down before them.
    The uplifted hands of men can touch Jupiter's heart   80
so that he stays the thunderbolt in his hand, and a small
    but honest offering may appease the gods.
He has long had it in mind to write to you, and love
    will not allow him further procrastination,
for he has heard rumors—which sometimes deliver the truth,
    especially if unpleasant—that where you live
there is civil disturbance, your city now besieged
    by ravaging armies for which the Saxons prepare.
Enyo, the goddess of war, has been devastating the fields
    far and wide, and blood now drenches the earth   90
in which for a grisly crop men's flesh has been relocated.
    Mars has abandoned Thrace and redirected

to Germany where he urges his warhorses to trample
  the whole world underfoot. The olive tree
withers, and Eirene, the goddess of peace who hates
  the harsh blast of the brazen trumpets flees.
Diké, the goddess of justice, has also removed herself
  to reside in heaven as Virgo. The horrors of war
surround you where, alone and a helpless stranger, you seek
  the protection and the sustenance you enjoyed   100
when you were living at home. How could such things happen
  that Englishmen should be driven out of their homes
for reasons of faith and conscience? A ruthless parent she is
  with a heart as hard as her famous white cliffs
where the waves beat on her shores. It does not at all become her
  thus to abandon her perfectly innocent children
and drive them into foreign dangers and discomforts.
  How can she suffer those whom God himself
appointed to bear glad tidings and teach the way that leads
  from death to an eternal life in heaven   110
to be forced to fend for themselves in remote and dangerous places?
  Those who have committed this outrage
should be consigned forever to dwell in Stygian darkness
  where they will perish from hunger of the soul!
Even so was Elijah forced by Jezebel
  and Ahab to flee and tread the lonely paths.
of desert wastes; thus was Paul of Tarsus, tortured
  and bleeding from the cruel lash, cast out
of Macedon; and thus did the Gadarenes send away
  Jesus from their city of ingrates.   120
But even so, take heart and do not allow your hopes
  to die within you. Do not permit your fears
to chill your bones' marrow. You are beset with soldiers
  in gleaming armor bearing their countless weapons,

but none of them shall even graze your defenseless breast,
and no spear point will drink your innocent blood.
You shall dwell in the perfect safety of God's protection.
He who overthrew the Assyrian host
beneath the walls of Zion and routed and put to flight
those whom Damascus had sent to Samarian fields   130
will be your protector. Remember how their great king trembled
and their cohort was stricken with universal terror
when out of the empty air the blare of trumpets sounded.
The pounding hoofs of their horses raised dust clouds
and the wheels of their fleeing chariots shook the sandy ground.
There was steel resounding on steel, and whinnying horses,
and the shouts and the harsh cries of men in the frenzy of battle.
Think of these things and keep your hopes alive,
while your spirit's courage defeats misfortune's empty threats.
Rely on the favor of the good God almighty   140
who will bring you to enjoy happier times than this
and allow you to return to your native ground."

The Fifth Elegy   *At the Age of Twenty*
On the Approach of Spring

Time in its endless circle brings around in season
    the welcome warmth of Zephyr's gentle breath.
The earth, rejuvenated, reacquires that bloom
    of youth that she and we had all but forgotten.
I am also refreshed and can almost persuade myself
    that a new strength comes to enliven my song
as the precious gift of springtime reinspires my talents.
    My powers at any rate become impatient
and demand the exertions that some challenging task might offer.
    I can see before my eyes twin-peaked Parnassus   10
and lower in the ravine the sweet limpid waters
    of the Muses' Castalian spring. In my dreams at night
I visit Macedon's Pierian fountain and drink
    of the knowledge it holds. I feel my burning heart
beat in a tumultuous rapture I cannot ignore.
    Phoebus himself appears before me, his hair
encircled by Daphne's laurel. My giddy mind is caught up
    in flights through the clouds and into the limpid heavens.
My spirit is borne through the shades to the dwelling places of poets,
    and the open shrines of the gods invite me to enter.   20
My soul understands the enterprise of Olympian gods
    and sees into the secrets Tartarus holds.
What splendor will issue forth to pour from my parted lips?
    Spring is my inspiration and I shall repay
his gifts with whatever tribute my heart and talent can work.
    Now Philomela, from your hiding place
in the leaves, you begin your song while the rest of the woodlands
    hush.
    I here in the city and you in the forest

will celebrate together the coming on of Spring.

　　See, he has returned, so let us praise 　　　　　　　　　　30

and honor him. Let the Muse resume her annual task.

　　The sun departs from his Ethiopian fastness

and with his golden reins directs his fiery car

　　northward and back to us who have been waiting.

Briefer now are the hours we have of night and darkness

　　and Boötes, the plowman now pursues the Plough[1]

at a lesser distance. The stars throughout the spangled heavens

　　keep watch at the court of Jove. Fraud, murder,

and violence diminish as the cover of night grow shorter.

　　The gods do not have to fear the giants' onslaughts. 　　　40

And a shepherd up on the ridge line, leaning against a boulder,

　　declares as the earth grows red in the rising sun:

"This is surely the night, O Phoebus, when you miss

　　that lovely one who restrains your galloping steeds."

Discerning the bright rays of the sun, his sister Cynthia

　　declines to shine with her lesser beams and gladly

returns to the forest to take up her bow and quiver of arrows,

　　thankful that she has been relieved from her watch.

"Come, Aurora," Phoebus cries, "and leave the chamber

　　of your agéd husband! To lie in a cold bed? 　　　　　　50

What joy can there be in that? Cephalus, Aeolis' son,

　　awaits you in the meadow in which he hunts."

With a blush upon her cheek the goddess admits her fault

　　and urges the horses of morning to greater speed.

Earth with its new life casts off enfeebling age

　　and is eager to receive Phoebus' caress

which she desires and of which she is indeed worthy,

　　for who is more fair than she when she bares her breast

---

1. The British name for the Big Dipper

touched with the delicate scents of Arabia's finest perfumes?
    She nourishes everything we see around us   60
and from her lips there pours the delicate fragrance of roses.
    Her lofty brow is crowned with a sacred wood
as a tower of pines encircles Ops on top of Mount Ida.
    She entwines her dew-moist hair with various flowers
with which she has learned to increase the heat of her lover's ardor,
    just as Proserpina with garlands of blossoms
enchanted the underworld's god. Look, O Phoebus, a willing
    love awaits you. The breezes of spring are laden
with prayers as sweet as honey. Zephyr now fans his wings
    that give off a cinnamon scent, while the twitter of birds   70
rises in songs of praise. Earth, who seeks your love,
    does not come empty-handed but brings her dower
of the potent herbs you use as a healer, treating sickness.
    If lavish gifts can arouse your interest (often
love can be bought with wealth), she lays before you treasures
    she has hidden beneath the depths of the sea
and under her mountains. Think how you bring the days to a close
    plunging headlong into the western waves:
how often have you heard her call out her plaintive appeals?
    "Why is it, O Phoebus, that when the day is done   80
it is the cerulean mother who always receives you? What
    have you to do with Tethys? What are waves
to you? Why should you want to bathe your divine face
    in Ocean's salty water? The coolness you want
you can more easily find in one of my shady glens.
    Come, dear Phoebus, cool your glowing locks
with the delicate dew I offer and enjoy a sweet repose
    as you lie on the soft cool grass. Come to me now
and lay your splendors upon my breast where a playful breeze
    will caress both of our bodies among the roses.   90

I am not at all frightened by Semele's terrible fate
    or the steeds you allowed Phaethon to drive.
When you have put your fires to better and wiser use,
    come and lie in pleasure upon my breast."
Thus does wanton Earth give voice to her powerful yearnings,
    and all her children model their behavior
following her example. Cupid wanders the world,
    rekindles his flaming torch in the sun's fire,
and strings again his deadly bow to fire those arrows
    the cruel points of which gleam in his quiver.   100
He even thinks of assaulting the immaculate Diana
    or virginal Vesta who sits by the sacred hearth.
Venus each year rejuvenates her aging body
    and seems to have risen again fresh from the sea.
Through the marble halls of cities young men sing their praises
    to Hymen that echo out in the country on seashores,
in caves, and on mountainsides, *Io, Hymen!* In splendid
    garb he arrives, his tunic fragrant with crocus.
Troops of maidens, their bodices belted in gold, go forth
    to the joys of the beautiful springtime, each one praying   110
her own prayer that resembles those of all the others—
    that Venus may grant each an attractive husband.
Now does the joyful shepherd pipe on his seven-reed syrinx
    and Phyllis responds to this with a suitable song.
The mariner greets the stars, singing his sweet chanteys
    to which the dolphins dance atop the waves.
Jupiter himself on the peak of Olympus, prompted
    to merriment with Juno, calls his attendant
gods and demigods to celebrate with a feast.
    As twilight falls, the nimble satyrs dance   120
across the flowery fields with cypress-crowned Silvanus.
    Dryads roam the mountains and lonely meadows

while Pan romps through thickets and over the tilth,
   pestering even Cybele and Ceres.
Faunus stalks a beautiful Oread who flees
   on trembling feet and hides but is ill hidden,
more than half-hoping that she may yet be found.
   The deities in this sweet season prefer the earth
to the dignity of heaven and many of them descend
   so that every grove and brook has its own god.   130
This is as it should be. Do not desert us, gods,
   but let the age of gold return and restore you
to this unhappy world! Why return to the clouds'
   wrangles and wars? At the very least, O Phoebus,
rein in your fleet horses and let the springtime pass
   mercifully slowly. Keep winter away
as long as you can with its protracted nights and darkness,
   when we endure the shadows that fall from the pole.

The Sixth Elegy
To Charles Diodati, Staying in the Country

While staying in the country, Diodati had written the author on 13 December and asked him to excuse his verses if they were not so good as usual, because, amid the festivities with which he had been received by his friends, he was unable to devote himself sufficiently to the Muses; he received the following reply.

Unsurfeited by feasting, I wish you a good health
    which you may need with your over-burdened stomach.
But why should your Muse engage with mine and rouse her
    from the shade she so much enjoys? Do you need song
to convince you how much I love and cherish you? Believe me,
    prose would work for that. My friendship is not
constrained by the rules of metrics. It marches along on feet
    that need not keep to elegiac lines.
How splendidly you recount the festivities of December,
    the banquets and the attendant merriment   10
in honor of the god who fled the comforts of heaven
    to appear on earth! How well do you describe
the joys of the wintertime out on a country estate,
    feasting and drinking wine by the fireside.
But why do you complain, when you know perfectly well
    that Song loves Bacchus and Bacchus, Song?
Phoebus was not ashamed to wear Bacchus' corymbus,
    that woven cluster of sporty ivy berries,
which he liked every bit as much as his own wreath of laurel.
    Often up in the hills have the nine Muses exclaimed   20
Evoë and mixed in with the Bacchanalian revels.
    The verses Ovid sent back from distant Tomis
were not quite up to his suave standard, and he had no
    delicacies there and wine to distract him.

What beside wine and roses did Anacreon celebrate?
  Bacchus inspired Pindar, and every page
breathes the fragrance of wine he drank while he was writing
  of chariot races and horsemen churning up dust
in Olympian races at Elis on the banks of the River Alph.
  Horace used to drink wine when he praised   30
Glycera the svelte brunette or Chloe the gorgeous blonde.
  The dapatical table and excellent wines are conducive
to the pouring out of verse as if from a crystal decanter,
  for to efforts made in this jovial manner Bacchus,
Apollo, and Ceres all together come to our aid.
  The quality of such verses is no surprise,
written with the support of three gods standing behind us.
  When a pretty hand sweeps the strings of the lute
that Orpheus played, embellished with delicate inlays of gold,
  and in tapestried rooms guides the sprightly maidens   40
as they tread the patterns of dances, let your Muse recall
  whatever inspiration such idle indulgence
prompts in your heart. Whenever you hear the ivory keys
  producing their tunes and the festive band joins in
to fill a perfumed salon with pleasing music, Apollo
  will steal into your breast in a sudden glow
that will penetrate all the way to the marrow of your bones.
  Through the nimble hands and eyes of the lutenist, Thalia
will find a way to invade and occupy your bosom.
  Can elegy be mere *vers de société*   50
when so many gods approve it and summon whomever they choose
  to try their hands and show what they can do?
Bacchus comes, and Erato, Ceres, Venus, and Cupid
  have shown themselves to be partial to such efforts.
And poets who comply with the wishes of these gods
  are free to imbibe old wine and gourmandize,

but he whose ambition it is to sing grave songs of wars
    and try to recount the workings of Jove in the world,
who celebrates the actions of heroes and demigods
    and the leaders of men, who explains the stern decrees   60
of the gods above or else of the realm below where the dog
    barks . . . He must live a spare and abstemious life
as Pythagoras did, abstaining from flesh and ingesting only
    leaves and herbs. His drink must be pure water
in a wooden bowl fresh from a bubbling spring. His youth
    must always be chaste and free from the taint of sin.
His manners must be correct and the deeds of his hand, blameless
    as that of the priest who approaches a god's altar.
This is how Tiresias lived in those difficult years
    after he was blinded, and Theban Linus,   70
and Calchas, who spoke the terrible words to the Greeks at Aulis.
    This was the regimen agèd Orpheus kept
when he was taming the wild beasts in their lonely caves.
    Homer, too, was sparing in matters of diet
and drank nothing but water in order that he could carry
    Odysseus over the wine-dark sea and to Circe's,
island, past the Sirens' shoals, and through the grim
    house of the underworld where he spilled dark blood
and thus was able to hold the crowds of shades spellbound.
    The bard is sacred to gods and serves as a priest   80
for his heart and lips express the thoughts of an indwelling Jove.
    If you want to know how I occupy myself—
if, indeed, such details as this are of any interest—
    I am singing now of the peace-bringing King of Heaven
and of that happy age that will come about one day
    as the sacred books foretold, and the infant cries
of the baby Jesus sheltered out in the inn's barn
    and who now dwells with his Father in realms above.

I sing of the great star and the hymns of the heavenly angels
   and of Greek and Roman gods undone in their shrines.   90
This is my gift: "On the Morning of Christ's Nativity,"
   for the first light of that dawn gave me my theme.
This I wrote in the strains of my native tongue and soon
   when we meet, I shall recite them and you will judge.

The Seventh Elegy
"Not yet, O Gentle Venus"

Not yet, O gentle Venus, had I studied your stern laws
    nor had my heart been singed by Cyprian[1] flames.
I therefore made light of Cupid's quiver of little arrows,
    which I dismissed as children's harmless playthings.
Worse than that, I failed to recognize the divine
    powers the god Amor can wield here in the world.
"Go on, little boy," is what I dared to say, "and shoot
    timid doves that are better suited as foes
and from whom you may more easily win your schoolyard triumphs.
    Make war, if you must, upon the bustling sparrows."   10
These taunts he could not endure, for he is as prompt to anger
    as any god and he burned with ire's fire.
It was spring, and the light poured over the roofs of the village.
    The glare of morning dazzled my poor eyes.[2]
And suddenly there he was, standing beside my bed,
    Love, unwearying Love with his painted wings.
His quiver made it perfectly clear who he was, and his face,
    the sweet face of a boy, but with threatening eyes.
Who else would have such beauty? Jupiter's Ganymede,
    who fills the cups of the gods? Or possibly Hylas,[3]   20
Theodamas' son, whom the Naiad snatched away,
    the Argonaut who disappeared in her fountain?
Cupid's beauty exceeded either of those and was such
    that his displeasure made him all the more gorgeous.
He addressed me with his threats and glared at me in the harshness
    my impolite behavior surely deserved:

1. At Amathus, in Cyprus, there was a temple sacred to Venus.
2. Some read this as a reference to the poet's weak eyes that eventually failed him.
3. An Argonaut who was, like Ganymede, famed for his beauty, and who was seized by a nymph.

"It would have been far better," he said with icy restraint,
  "if you had been able to learn from others' pains
the extent of my powers. But now, you shall yourself bear witness
  to what my right hand is able to do.   30
You shall be one of my victims whose story men will recount,
  thereby spreading my fame and confirming their faith.
Do you not recall how I conquered Apollo, proud
  after he had slain the mighty Python?[4]
I shot him with my golden arrow and he was in love
  at once with Peneus' beautiful daughter Daphne,
whom I had also shot but with my arrow of lead
  so that she was altogether unwilling!
Phoebus now admits that the wounds of my arrows are worse
  than any of his. The famous Parthian bowmen   40
who kill as they flee can shoot with no greater skill than mine.
  And Cephalus, the Cretan hunter, pays me
regretful respect, having killed Procris, his dear wife.
  Burly Orion[5] I vanquished, and Hercules too,
and Telamon his friend. Not even mighty Jove
  is immune to the effects of my sharp darts.
But whatever doubts you may still have will be laid to rest
  not by mere words but dramatic deeds,
as I aim for your heart's target. Your Muses cannot defend you,
  nor can the twin serpents of Apollo's   50
healing arts[6] cure you or assuage your grievous pains."
  Then he flew away to his Cyprian mother
to hide in her warm bosom. I'm sorry to say I laughed
  at the boy's threats that I mistook for bluster.

---

4. Exulting in his victory over the Python, Apollo scorned Cupid, who struck him with a golden dart to arouse his love for Daphne.

5. Orion, the giant, was a mighty hunter who violated Merope in Chios.

6. The serpents that coil about the medical Caduceus, which refers to Asculapius' appearing in Rome in the form of a snake to end the pestilence there.

I went about my business, or rather say my pleasures,
    now in the city center, and now in the towns
out in the countryside. And everywhere I went
    there seemed to be great crowds of attractive people
as if a bevy of nymphs or of goddesses had gathered
    here in our streets on a beautiful spring morning,   60
one of those days when Phoebus seems to be able to bask
    in the splendors that his rays have accomplished here.
My spirits were high and my youthful ardor led me along,
    so that my eyes met theirs, and I was caught.
I could not look away. And of course I noticed one
    whose beauty clearly surpassed that of the others.
She returned my glance and that, I am certain now, was the start
    of all my ills. If Venus chose to appear
to mortals, this was the form that she might be pleased to take.
    Or put it the other way and say that Venus,   70
the beautiful queen of the gods, must have looked like her.
    It was Cupid's mischievous plan to put her there,
to make good his threat, ensnare me, and teach me a lesson.
    In fact he was there, lurking close by, his quiver
full of arrows swinging across his diminutive back
    and holding his torch high above his head.
He flitted across her face, clinging now to her eyelids
    and now to the full lips of her pretty mouth,
before he settled at last on the curve of her rosy cheek.
    From each of these points he shot another arrow   80
every one of them wounding my poor defenseless breast.
    Instantly, strange passions filled my heart
and the fire of love I had never known before consumed me.
    I was paralyzed with my ardor, all aflame,
but she to whom I had given my heart and soul disappeared,
    snatched away never to reappear.

In deepest grief and silence, I wandered about at random,
  my understanding dulled, my will gone.
Often I retraced my steps hoping to find her.
  I was torn asunder, my body in one place,   90
but my soul elsewhere, pursuing the object of my desire
  and taking cold comfort in shedding tears
for all the joys I had lost even before I had known them.
  Thus did Vulcan mourn his loss of heaven,
cast down as he was by Jove among the hearths of Lemnos.
  Thus did Amphiaraus also lament
as the earth beneath him swallowed his chariot and horses
  so that the sun above him suddenly vanished.
What shall I do now, wretched and overcome
  with grief? I cannot pursue my lost love,   100
nor put it aside. I yearn to behold her face once again.
  To see her, to speak only a word or two,
face to face . . . Perhaps she would not be deaf to my prayers.
  No one has ever suffered such pains as mine!
Love is said to be tender. Spare me, then, O god!
  Let your behavior suit your reputation
for sweetness. I now concede the power of your sharp shafts,
  no less fearsome than fire. Your bow as well
is a terrifying weapon. Henceforth your altars will smoke
  with offerings I shall make to you in worship.   110
Take my longings away and my pain. Or, no,
  do not! I find my agonies somehow sweet.
But I pray to you that someday a maiden will come to be mine
  as both of us are pierced by a single arrow.

This is what in my feckless youth, with my true zeal
  put aside, I wrote, souvenirs of worthlessness.
Utterly full of error, they show me led astray,
  my untaught youth needing a better teacher.

But the shades of Academe in which Socratic streams
   flow were just what I needed to unlearn   120
my error and loose the heavy yoke from my bowed neck.
   My heart is cooler now, and Venus' shafts
are harmless against me: she dreads my new-found strength,
   almost the equal of mighty Diomedes'.

The Epigrams

On the Gunpowder Plot

O, sly Guy Fawkes, you plotted against your king
 and the British lords, but did you intend to be kind
and make up for your malice in this thing
 with at least a show of piety? Do we find
an intention, perhaps, of sending the members of court
 up to the sky in a chariot made of fire
the way Elijah traveled. Or do I distort
 the simple wickedness of your desire?

On the Same

The Apocalypse's beast in the city of seven
hills pretends it can send King James to heaven.
Its false promise falls on our deaf ears,
now that the king, in the fullness of his years,
has departed thither. Better that it should rend
its cowls and smash its statues that cannot ascend
skyward unless they are burned to ash and smoke,
for otherwise Rome's promise is a joke.

On the Same

Godless Rome consigned James to the Styx,
but they've had second thoughts and are keen to see
him raised to heaven, although this contradicts
their earlier view. It beats the hell out of me.

On the Inventor of Gunpowder

The ancients praised Prometheus who brought
celestial fire to earth. But man has made
much progress. It appears that we have caught
up: Jove's lightning puts him in the shade.

To Leonora, Singing at Rome

Each man has his angel from the flights
of heaven's hierarchy. What wonder then
if your voice proclaims God's glory on the nights
when you perform here in the world of men.
We are spellbound and ask what higher power
breathes through your song to teach our mortal hearts.
God is in everything, but for this hour
He comes to us clearly through your voice's arts.

To the Same

Another woman bearing the same name
aroused in Tasso a passion that drove him mad,
which was, the world must agree a terrible shame.
How much better for him and for us if he had
fallen for you. Had he heard your sweet
voice, it would have cured him, restoring his wits.
Even if his derangement had been complete,
your harmony would have composed his mind and its
function and his senses could have been saved
as you calmed his great spirit that merely raved.

Fable of the Peasant and the Landlord

A certain peasant gathered every fall
the finest apples from his apple tree
to bring to his master who lived in town—a small
but welcome gift. The landlord greedily
transplanted the tree to his own garden where
he'd have all the apples he wanted. In the field
the old tree had managed somehow to bear
but now it withered and could no longer yield
fruit. The landlord saw how he had erred,
and cursed the work of his hands and also his greed:
"My tenant's gift were adequate to my need,
To want more was unseemly and absurd."

On Salmasius

O fish, rejoice, swimming about in the sea,
and thank Salmasius among whose concerns
is your nakedness in the winter's frigidity.
He makes clothing for you whenever he turns
out another sonnet or villanelle
(with his crest on top of the page). These you will wear
as your outer garments, for those good men who sell
fish will use them to wrap you for customers there.

The Book
of the Woods

On the Death of the Vice Chancellor, a Physician
At the Age of Sixteen

Learn to submit to destiny's laws
and lift your hands as suppliants to fate,
    O children of Heaven and Earth.
    Our legacy at birth

was mortality, for we all wait
for death to call. No stratagems
    or tricks that we may play
    will make him delay.

Each of us must cross the Styx.
Were mere strength enough to deter   10
    death, then for Heracles
    there'd have been no obsequies

when he was poisoned by Nessus' blood.
Neither would mighty Hector at Troy
    have been so cruelly slain
    by Athena's legerdemain.

Sarpedon could not have been struck down
by the Locrian Patroclus, wearing
    Achilles' armor, who strove
    against a son of Jove.   20

If magic words could frustrate death,
wicked Circe would still be alive
    and Medea, casting some spell,
    would be alive and well.

If mysterious herbs and nostrums were
weapons that worked to fend off the Fates,
　　Machaon would not fear
　　Eurypylus' sharp spear.

Chiron the centaur, saved the life
of the infant in Coronis' womb,   30
　　but Heracles' blood-smeared dart
　　struck him and stopped his heart.

And you, Dr. Gostlin, who were as great
as your master and tutor Apollo, to whom
　　was entrusted the health of gowned
　　men, would not lie in the ground.

All Cambridge mourns you, and Helicon's
springs are weeping at your loss.
　　You should be with us still,
　　attending well to the ill.   40

You would never have boarded Charon's skiff
to sail with him into the abyss.
　　But Persephone was irked
　　by the many cures you had worked,

and the many souls you had snatched back
by your arts from the gaping jaws of death.
　　Reverend Chancellor, you
　　should have what is your due:

from your grave may marigolds,
roses, and hyacinths spring,   50

and may Aeacus be just
when he comes to judge your dust;

may Proserpine smile upon
your spirit, now that you're gone.
    In Elysium, may you rest
    forever among the blessed.

On the Fifth of November
At the Age of Seventeen

Hardly had the pious James come down from the north
to assume the rule of the people of Albion who had sprung
from ancient Trojan blood; hardly had the treaty
joined together the English and Scottish crowns and scepters,
with the king, in peace and wealth and happiness, taking his place
on the new throne, secure from foes, open or secret,
when the terrible tyrant, the father of Furies, the wandering exile
from Olympus' majestic heights who rules Acheron's flood
chanced to rove about the immense orb of the earth
to tally up his faithful slaves and companions in evil   10
who, when they are buried, will take their place in his realm.
Hovering here in midair, he rouses terrible tempests
and scatters among like-minded friends the seeds of hatred.
He appeals to the pride of nations that think they cannot be
        conquered
to wage war against others that labor under the same
dangerous misconception. Where the olive of peace thrives,
he creates confusion that leads to tumult and mortal combat.
Whoever devotes himself to decency and to virtue
he beguiles with deceptions, corrupting their temptingly innocent
        hearts.
He knows how to lay his snares and spread his treacherous nets   20
that entangle unwary men whom he delights to capture
and whom he follows as silent as any Caspian tiger
relentlessly stalking its trembling prey through pathless wastes
on a moonless night ill lit by the furtive twinkle of stars.
With such destructive intent does the underworld god Summanus,
girt with whirling smoke and flickers of blue-white flame,
appear to overwhelm the cities and towns of men.
He sees the famous beetling cliffs with their skirts of foam,

and the land the sea-god loves enough so that his son
who ruled here bestowed his name upon it—Albion.   30
Summanus saw the fertile and peaceful fields that Ceres
had blessed and, what was worse, a people who gave their thanks
and praise to the one true god. This provoked him sorely
to sighs and groans with eruptions of Tartarean flames and brimstone,
sulfurous and lurid, like those of the monster Typhoeus
whom Jove consigned beneath Mount Aetna that belches forth
from its noisome mouth expressions of burning hatred and rage.
His eyes are aglow with sinister flashes and from his jaws
there come the sounds of his gnashing teeth that sound like weapons,
lance meeting iron armor or sword smashing on shield.   40
    "This," he said, "is as dreadful as anything I have yet seen
as I have wandered the world. This nation alone rejects me
and spurns my powerful yoke and all my machinations.
If my efforts can accomplish what I now have in mind,
they shall not long defy me without paying the cost
that I shall impose on them who will know my vengeance."
    Thus he spoke and on pitch-black wings he soared through the air,
and wherever he flew there were mighty headwinds that came before
        him,
accumulations of thick clouds and flashes of lightning.
He passed over the peaks of the snowy Alps and reached   50
Italy where, on the left, the stormy Apennines lie,
the land of the ancient Sabines, and opposite, on the right,
Tuscany, notorious for sorcerers and magi.
He passed the Tiber that flows through Rome to kiss the sea
and descended to Romulus' city where, in the fading twilight,
he beheld the man who wears the triple crown on a litter
carried about in streets on the shoulders of burly men
and bearing their bread-made gods. Before him were kings on their
        knees
and an endless line of mendicant friars carrying tapers.

All of them blind fools, thus dragging out their lives   60
in Cimmerian darkness! They entered their temple, bright with
    torches,
for it was St. Peter's Day. Thunders of songs and chants
rose to resound in the domes in a Bacchic enthusiasm
that once used to fill the air of Boeotian Mount Aracynthus
while the River Asopus trembled and from far away Mount Cithaeron
returned an echoing answer from one of its hollow cliffs.
When the solemn pomp of these rites came at last to an end,
it was time for Night to depart from Erebus' embrace
and urge her steeds headlong across the bowl of the sky—
Typhlos (blind), fierce Melanchaetes (having black hair),   70
Siope (silence), and long-maned Phryx (one who shudders).

    The subduer of kings, meanwhile, the proud pontifical heir
to the throne where fiery Phlegethon flows, had entered his chamber,
for he does not pass his nights without some concubine,
but sleep had barely closed his eyes when the lord of the shades
appeared in a false form and stood close to his bedside.
His temples were silvered and gray and a white beard hung to his
    breast;
a garment of ashen hue swept the ground where he walked;
a hood covered his head and concealed his face in its shadow;
and, lest he give himself away, his loins were bound   80
with a cord of hemp. Slowly in sandaled feet he approached . . .
so had Francis walked alone in the desert sands
among the haunts of the wild beasts, a sinner who brought
to the dumb creatures pious words of the world's salvation
and thus he had managed to gentle the wolves and the Libyan lions.

    In this disguise the deceiver addressed the recumbent pope,
speaking these inveigling words from his hateful lips:
"Are you asleep, my son? Does your fatigue overpower
your body's limbs? You forget your faith as well as your flock!
Even now, as I speak, there are, far to the north,   90

barbarian people defying your throne and your triple crown!
The quivering Britons scorn the laws of the holy father.
Bestir yourself! Arise from your sloth! Remember how
the emperor adores you! Think of the keys of heaven
that you have in your hands to make those gates fly open!
Break their shameless pride and rebellious spirits and show
how sacrilege fares in the world when you have pronounced your
    curses.
Avenge the defeat of the Spanish fleet where their flags drifted
slowly down to the tranquil bed of the cruel sea.
Think of the saints and martyrs that Amazon virgin queen   100
sent to hang on the gallows or to lay their heads on the block.
If you lie there on your soft bed pillows, fail to act,
and refuse to encounter the foe while his strength every day increases,
the enemy soon will fill the sea with his ships and soldiers
and plant his haughty standard atop the Aventine hill.
He will smash the holy relics and fling them into the flames
and tread with his infidel feet upon the nape of your neck,
even if kings have been delighted to kiss your feet.
But do not attempt any direct attack which could fail;
rather make use of fraud and guile, bearing in mind   110
that such actions are right and proper for heretics.
Their king has summoned to council the kingdom's dignitaries
the hereditary peers from everywhere in the land,
and the white-haired sages as well in their fine robes of state.
All these you can blast to ashes with a little well-placed powder
underneath the buildings in which they are all convened.
But before you take such action, you must give fair warning
to whatever souls have remained steadfast in their faith.
These will surely obey your instructions and keep away
and therefore be spared from any harm in the great explosion.   120
Then, when the nation is seized with panic and in confusion,
let the ruthless Gauls fall upon them or else

the Iberian hordes that are eager to invade and annex their land.
Thus will the spirit return of the age of the faithful Queen Mary
and you will regain your rule over the valiant English.
Fear naught; dread naught; but trust in all the gods and saints
that you parade through the streets on your many festival days!"

So the fiend spoke and then, putting aside his costume,
disappeared forthwith to the joyless realm of Lethe.

The doorman of the celestial hall had driven away   130
sleep and the nocturnal shapes of pleasant dreams
when rosy-fingered dawn emerged from the eastern gates
to tinge the earth again with a fresh and gentle light,
while weeping dewy tears down on the mountain tops
for the death of her son Memnon before the walls at Troy.

There is a place obscured by the darkness of constant night
where in the vast foundations of ruined buildings lurk
cruel Murder and double-tongued Treachery, the twins
Discord brought forth. Here in their dismal den
among the broken rocks are unburied bones of men   140
and rotting corpses pierced and gashed by cold steel.
Here sits Guile with his furtive eyes and also Strife
and Calumny with those fangs protruding from his jaw.
And Fury, and Death in a thousand different forms, and Fear
also dwell here, and Horror flying through murky air,
and bodily shapes cry out to punctuate the silence.
The very earth is ashamed, moist as it is with blood.
There, deep in a cave, Murder and Treason sit
where no one dares approach through the hall of jagged rocks,
and there the guilty pair cower, but even so,   150
Babylon's high priest can command them as he pleases,
for they have been loyal and faithful servants to him for years.

"On the very western edge of the world," he tells the two,
"surrounded by ocean there lives a people whom I detest,
smug on their little island, aloof from the rest of the world.

Go there at once, I command you, and find among the faithful
associates in my plot and aids in its execution.
Then, with infernal power of powder, let them be blown
sky high, the king, the nobles, and the entire accursèd race."
    With these words, he fell silent, and the ruthless twins at once   160
hurried to carry out his orders. The Lord of Heaven
who turns the sphere of the heavens and sends down lightning bolts
from his citadel on high, looked down with a sad smile
at the efforts of this perverse crown that would be in vain
as long as he himself was defending his people's cause.
    Somewhere equidistant from Europe and Asia, there stands
high on a mountain the lofty Tower of Fame, where the Titan
goddess dwells. A thousand windows and doors gape wide
and from spacious courtyards within a murmuring crowd mills,
buzzing like so many flies where the milk pails are set out.   170
At the highest point sits Fame and she perks her numberless ears
with which she gathers whispers of rumors from everywhere.
Not even you, Argus, the unreliable guard
of Io, rolled so many eyes in your savage face.
Fame's eyes never get drowsy but she gazes far and wide
over the landscape below, even into the darkness,
places in which the rays of the sun don't ever shine.
Whatever she sees or hears, her babbling tongue pours out,
utterly disregarding the truth of what she says,
exaggerating or minimizing as it may please her.   180
Fame, nevertheless, deserves praise in our song
for her one good deed, than which there could not be a better.
I am proud to honor her here, and I do not apologize
for going on at some length—for she was the savior of England.
Capricious goddess, we offer our deepest gratitude.
God, who tempers the motion of stars and planets, hurled
his thunderbolt and, while the earth still trembled, said:
    "Are you silent now, O Fame? Or are you unaware

of the evil band of Papists conspiring now against me
and against my people, the Britons? Have you not heard the
    news   190
of the terrible murder that they are planning against King James?"
    She heard and accepted these commands of the Thunderer God
and even though she was normally speedy, now she hastened
to put on her buzzing wings and clothe her body in plumage.
In her right hand she held a shining brazen trumpet
as she beat the air with her wings and outstripped all the clouds,
and even the winds which she left behind, and the sun's horses.
Through all the English cities and towns she spread her tales—
uncertain, even contradictory, but disturbing,
and growing ever louder—of the men who were plotting
    together   200
this treacherous act. She spoke of the deed itself but included
the names of those involved as well as the place and time
that they had settled upon. Young men and pretty maidens,
and worn old men and women were seized with great alarm
at the thought of such a disaster that struck deep in their hearts.
Meanwhile, the Heavenly Father on high was moved to pity
for these, his people, and he thwarted the Papists' plans:
the conspirators were captured and dragged away to justice.
Honors and incense were offered as signs of gratitude
for the nation's having been spared. At all the crossroads, fires   210
of celebration burned, and young men and women danced,
and no day more than the Fifth of November sees such rejoicing.

On the Death of the Bishop of Ely

At the Age of Seventeen

My cheeks were still wet from my flood of salty
    tears and my eyes were still red
and puffy from all that weeping at the bier
    of the highly esteemed Bishop of Winchester
when hundred-tongued Fame, whose news of misfortune
    and evil always turns out to be true,
spread throughout the cities of rich Britain
    and among the people sprung from Neptune
the report that you, an honor to all mankind
    and chief of the saints of Ely's island,   10
had yielded at last to Death and the fatal sisters.
    Anger surged at once through my breast
and I cursed the powerful goddess who rules over graves.
    Ovid's litany of invectives
in the *Ibis* were no more dreadful or damning than mine.
    The insults Archilochus hurled
against Lycambes that caused him and his daughters
    to go and hang themselves were mild
compared to those that bubbled up in my mind.
    But while I spoke these execrations,   20
invoking destruction upon the arch-destroyer,
    I was startled to hear these sounds borne
on the breeze in the mild and oddly gentle air:
    "Put away anger; put away
your empty and impotent threats. Those powers you curse
    cannot be hurt but may be annoyed.
Death is not, as it seems that you suppose,
    the black daughter of Night, nor of Erebus,
nor of the Erinys living below in Chaos.
    She has been sent from the starry heavens   30

to gather from throughout the world God's harvest.
     She calls forth into the air
and light the souls the body has hidden away,
     even as the fleeting Hours,
the daughters of Themis and Jove, call forth the day.
     She leads the Righteous before the face
of our Eternal Father, but the wicked she hurls
     down to Tartarus' mournful realm
and abodes in the gloom deep beneath the earth.
     I rejoiced when I heard her call   40
and hastened at once to abandon my foul prison
     and among the angelic hosts
be happily borne to the stars that shine on high
     just as in ancient times the agèd
Elijah was carried away and up into heaven
     riding that chariot of fire.
Of the icy constellation of Boötes
     and the terrible Scorpion's claws,
and Orion with his sword I had no fear.
     I flew beyond the gleaming orb   50
of the sun and I saw the moon below my feet,
     as that golden triform goddess
checked her dragons tugging on golden reins.
     Through the ranks of wandering stars
and through the Milky Way I was borne along
     at a speed beyond comprehension
until I came to the gates atop Olympus
     through which I passed and then beheld
a crystal palace, its forecourt paved with jasper.
     But here, I fear, I have to stop   60
for no man born of a mortal can begin to describe
     the delights I shall enjoy forever."

That Nature Does Not Suffer from Old Age   *1628?*

Alas, the vagrant mind of man begins to grow weary
in its endless struggle with error. Overwhelmed by darkness
it wanders about in a night as black as what Oedipus knew.
Absurdly, it presumes to judge the acts of the gods
by the rules it has invented to weigh its own behavior,
and tries to compare the adamantine laws of nature
to those that legislatures have enacted here on earth
and it attempts to fathom within the brief span of its days
that plan of fate which is unchanging and eternal.
   Does Nature wither and age? Is her brow furrowed with
     wrinkles?   10
Does the great mother of all creatures and things decline
into an age in which her womb is closed and barren?
Must she dodder with uncertain steps? Does her starry head
nod and even tremble? Do the years' hungers and thirsts
enfeeble her? Shall gluttonous Time swallow heaven
and devour his own father? This is exactly the evil
that mighty Jove tried to forestall in his citadels.
He wanted not to submit to the ravages of Time.
He wanted the stars and planets to whirl in their proper orbits
forever. And yet someday, the floor of heaven will tremble   20
and crumble and then, with a thunderous roar, all things shall fall
in ruins with the poles of the earth collapsing. Jove
shall tumble down from his celestial palace and with him
Athena too with her famous Gorgon shield uncovered—
just as Vulcan fell from heaven to crash upon Lemnos.
Phoebus, you shall imitate Phaeton's sad fate
and plunge in sudden ruin with your brilliant lamp extinguished.
The Old Man of the Sea shall give off a fearsome hissing
with a crashing of huge waves. With their summits undermined,
the Balkans shall heave and tumble. The Ceraunian hills as well   30

that Pluto threw at the giants will fall to his Stygian realm.

And yet the omnipotent Father who fixed the stars in their courses
gave thought to the sum of things and adjusted the scales of the fates
to weigh with a certain balance. It was He who ordained that all
      things
in magnificent order should move in their predetermined paths
forever, and thus, does the prime wheel of the universe turn
in its daily round, bearing with it the spheres of heaven.
Saturn moves no slower or faster than is his wont,
and radiant Mars gleams where he should in his crested helmet.
Phoebus shines with the bloom of perpetual youthfulness   40
through the course that has been prescribed. He does not scorch the
      earth
by downward deviations but maintains his altitude
emitting his friendly light. The beautiful morning star
ascends from the east in fragrant India to summon
the ethereal flocks of Olympus, and then, as the evening star,
to call them home again as she parts the realm of time
with her twofold light. The moon waxes and then wanes,
enfolding the sky in the outstretched arms of her two horns.
The elements remain steadfast although, with a crash,
lightning smites the rocks and splits huge boulders asunder.   50
With a sound every bit as fierce the howling northwest wind
rages through the void, and the northeast, with equal force,
assails the warlike Scythians as it ushers winter in,
herding the dark clouds. Neptune continues to strike
Sicily's Capo di Faro as Triton sounds his conch.
The Balearic islands bear on their backs the bulk
of the hundred-armed Aegaeon. But the earth persists and endures.
Narcissus keeps his perfume. Cythera, Cyprus' youth
whom Phoebus Apollo loves, remains as handsome as ever.
Aware though she was of the great greed of mankind, earth   60
did not hide all her gold and gems under the mountains

or deep in the sea. For ages, the order of things has remained
unbroken and it shall continue until the last days' flames
Peter spoke of consume the world from pole to pole
and the huge arch of heaven becomes its funeral pyre.

The Platonic Idea as Understood by Aristotle

Tell us, O goddesses guarding the sacred groves, and you,
Memory, blessed mother of the nine Muses, and you,
Eternity, who lies at ease in some faraway cave,
guarding the unchanging acts and edicts of Jove,
recording heaven's feast days and the daily life of the gods!
Say who is the first incorruptible being,
immortal, eternal, and thus coeval with heaven, one
and yet universal, made in the very likeness of God—
that being after whose image Nature has fashioned men.
Surely, he does not dwell unborn in the mind of Jove   10
and thus is no twin of the virgin Pallas Athena.
However generalized his nature may be, he exists,
an individual unto himself in a portion of space.
Conceivably he wanders among the perdurable stars
and the ten spheres of heaven. Or else he lives on the moon,
that heavenly body closest to earth. Or perhaps he drowses
by Lethe's banks among the shades that are waiting for bodies
in which they may return to earth. Or does he wander in some
distant regions of earth, this archetype of a man
who walks as a huge giant, his head high in the skies   20
so as to frighten the gods, larger even than Atlas
who bears up the firmament? The Theban seer whose blindness
gave him profounder insight into the nature of things
could not in the depths of his metaphysical vision perceive him.
Mercury with his swift wings as he flew through the night
did not reveal to him his wise and learned prophets.
Sanchuniathon, the priest of Assyria, could recite
the entirety of Ninus' long ancestral line
and knew the secrets of Baal and all of Osiris' rites,
but he did not know this being. And Hermes Trismegistus,   30
skilled as he was in the arcane secrets of many religions,

left the idea to the priests and worshipers of Isis.
But you, the Academy's glory, the first to introduce
such monsters into the schools, surely you will remember
how you banished all the poets from your state.
You are the greatest of all inventors of fiction, and you,
admitting this, must join the poets in their exile.

To My Father

My wish is that the Pierian fountain's waters might flood
my breast and that the Castalian stream flowing down the slopes
of Parnassus might wet my lips so that my Muse could rise
from the trivial strains to which I have often turned my attention
and fly on adventurous wings to honor my reverend father.
I haven't the least idea whether the verses I write
will please your discerning eye, but I cannot imagine what else
could better serve to repay in some small part your gifts—
for which there is no adequate way of expressing my thanks.
No empty words could equal my feeling of obligation.   10
This page, nevertheless, displays all my resources
and my small horde of talent is here on these pieces of paper.
There is nothing I possess except what golden Clio
has given me, what my dreams have brought to me from the caves
of sleep, and what the laurel groves of the sacred wood
in the shade of Mount Parnassus have seen fit to bestow.
    Do not scorn the poet's song. These works are divine
for they reveal more than anything else our ethereal nature
and heavenly heritage. Nothing else in its origin shows
the mysterious workings of grace in the human mind that displays   20
still some small but sacred trace of Promethean fire.
The gods have a special fondness for song, which is able to move
even the trembling depths of Hades and melt the hearts
of the desperate shades and the cruel gods of the underworld.
Apollo's priestesses and Sibyls express themselves
in song when they disclose to us what the future holds.
At the sacred altars, the priest composes his verses whether
he sacrifices a bull that tosses its golden horns
or consults the reeking entrails for hints of destiny's purpose.
When I return to my home on Olympus and see the changeless   30
ages of eternity stretching out before me,

I shall enter the temples of heaven adorned with gold, singing
my sweet songs to the gentle strum of the ivory plectrum
with which the stars in the arches of heaven shall resound.
Even now, although we cannot hear it, the spirit
that encircles the swift bodies in orbit himself sings
along with the starry choirs in ineffable harmony,
while the Serpent's constellation's angry hiss is stilled.
Fierce Orion, turning tranquil, lowers his sword
and Atlas is relieved of the burden his shoulders bear.   40

    Before there was any sybaritic and showy feasting
and back when there was only temperate drinking of wine,
the banquets of kings were graced by the recitations of bards
who sat at the dinner table with their flowing locks encircled
by garlands of oak, and they used to chant the feats of heroes
and all their mighty deeds, or else they would sing of chaos
and how the broad foundations that underlie the world
came to be created by creeping gods that fed
on berries and acorns, before the thunderbolts were brought
from the cavern under Aetna. But what can music alone   50
accomplish without the words and the meaning of verse's numbers?
Sylvan choirs perhaps can content themselves with this
but for Orpheus it wasn't the lute alone but the song
that held the rivers back, gave the oak trees ears,
and moved the shades of the dead to shed tears of the living
as they comprehended the passionate utterance of his mouth.

    Do not dismiss the sacred Muses' efforts; think
not that they are vain or poor but the source of all
settings of words to fitting music. They are trained
to vary the vocalise through a thousand modulations.   60
With your talent, you deserve to be the heir of Arion,
the great harper who first devised the dithyramb.
If I was born a poet, why should it seem strange
that we, so closely joined by the loving bond of blood,

should pursue related arts and similar ways of living?
Apollo, wishing that he could divide himself in twain,
gave some of his gifts to me and others to you,
so that we, father and son, comprise the divided god.

    You pretend to disesteem the gentle Muses, but I
cannot believe you hate them. You did not direct my steps   70
to the broad way that leads to the fields of gain and money
and to men who hope to acquire their sacks of glittering gold.
You did not drag me off to the bar and the laws of the land
(so poorly observed) to condemn my delicate ears with wrangles
and foolish disputations. Instead, you indulged your son
and allowed my already nurtured mind to continue to grow
ever more rich and strong in retreats from the city's uproar
and pass my pleasant leisure hours by pastoral streams,
a happy companion or even the acolyte of Apollo.

    I pass over in silence (as Cicero used to say)   80
the common kindnesses of any loving parent,
for greater matters demand mention and my attention.
When at your cost I became fluent in Romulus' tongue
and mastered the graces of Latin as well as the lofty words
of the splendid Greeks (which became the lips of Jove himself),
you urged me to add to this florilegium more blossoms:
the harvest of Gallic gardens and even Italian weeds,
admittedly degenerate but not without their tang,
as well as the stately phrases in which the ancient prophets
of Palestine held forth. And beyond all that, you set me   90
on the path of study of all the secrets of heaven and earth,
whatever flows in the air or is hidden beneath the waves.
All this I learn through you, if only I make the effort,
and the parted clouds will reveal the naked beauties of science
offering her face to my adoring kisses—
unless I am too timid about what they could mean
and flee rather than undergo the risk of passion.

Let fools go in search of wealth who prefer the undemanding
riches of Austria's mines or those of far-off Peru.
Nothing is better than learning: my father's gift to me   100
could not have been more precious. Jove if he had granted
all but heaven could not have been any more lavish.
He who gave Hyperion's blazing chariot's reins
and its radiant light and tiara to Phaethon his son
could not—even if they were safe—have matched these gifts to me.
Therefore, since I am one, although the least and last,
of the company of scholars, I shall sit among ivy
and laurel, with the leaves of which victors are crowned
and mix in no more with the dull and vulgar rabble. My feet
will avoid the gaze of profane and uncomprehending eyes.   110
Sleepless cares, away, and away with all complaints!
The glance of naked envy and the sidelong goatish leer
I shall take as praises. Calumny, keep still!
You may close your serpent's jaws, which I do not at all fear.
All of you tormenters, begone, away, avaunt.
None of you can hurt me: I am not under your law,
and I may walk secure from the threat of your viper strikes.
    But as for you, dear father, since I cannot repay
your generous gifts to me nor begin recompense
with any deeds of mine, let it be sufficient   120
that I remember and with great thankfulness count over
in a faithful mind each one of your many kindnesses.
    And you, my youthful verses, my first feeble attempts,
if you hope to survive your master's pyre and thus endure
for endless years, and if oblivion's grasping paw
does not drag you down to Orcus, do you remember
and cherish these praises of mine for a splendid father
whose name and fame will be an exemplar for later ages.

To Salzilli, the Roman Poet, When He Was Ill   *1638–39*

O Muse who can, whenever the moment
calls for it, limp in the gait of Vulcan[1]
and be as pleasing as Deiopea,
the nymph who danced before Juno's couch,
come now and bear these few words
to Salzilli, whose extravagant praise
compared me to Homer, Virgil, and Tasso.
To this, Milton, a native of London,
a region in which the worst of winds
with raging lungs drives gusty blasts   10
swift and unbridled across the sky,
he who has come to the fruitful fields
of Italy to see its cities
of proud renown and encounter the genius
of its young men of wit and learning,
this same Milton writes to wish
complete good health for your ailing body
whose vessels are troubled with too much bile
that spreads disease through all your vitals.
That vile bile ought to have spared you   20
for all your dexterous verse in Sapphics
that poured forth from your Roman lips.
    O sweet gift of the gods, Health,
the sister of Hebe, goddess of youth,
and you, Phoebus—or rather Paean
if that name better suits you here—

Giovanni Salzilli wrote an extravagant quatrain praising Milton's poetry, to which this is his reply.

    1. The poem is in Scazontes, a modification of iambic trimeter in which a spondee or trochee takes the place of the final iambus, producing the halting effect that comes from ending on what feels like the wrong stress. Milton's metrics are ambitious but wobbly. I have done the poem in iambic tetrameter in order to avoid driving myself and my readers crazy.

ever since you slew the Python
you have been disease's foe,
know this man as your devoté.
You groves of Rome and gentle hills   30
among which Evander[2] chose to settle,
if any of our healing plants
should put forth curative blossoms or leaves,
let them each strive to be the first
to bring relief to this sick poet.
Restored, he will return to the Muses
and delight the plain with his sweet song.
King Numa's spirit shall be delighted
in the dark groves where he takes his eternal
leisure, reclining, his gaze fixed   40
on his dear Egeria,[3] mourning forever.
Tiber will be charmed by his songs
and indulge the annual hopes of the farmers.
With neither too little nor too much
water he will keep to his banks
and leave the kings in their sepulchers safe;
he will behave well and control
himself until he reaches the salt
coast and the temple there of Portunus.[4]

2. Evander, the son of Hermes and an Arcadian nymph, came to Italy some sixty years before the Trojan War and was hospitably received by Turnus.

3. Numa was the second of Rome's legendary kings. He married the nymph Egeria, who, when he died, fled the city and hid herself in the forests where her lamentations disturbed the rites of Diana.

4. Portunus was the god of harbors. His temple stood at the mouth of the Tiber, and the Romans prayed there for a safe return from their voyages.

Manso

Giovanni Batista Manso, marquis of Villa, is a man in the first rank of re-
nown among the Italians by reason not merely of his genius in literary pur-
suits, but also of his military valor. There is extant a dialogue on friendship
addressed to him by Torquato Tasso, whose devoted friend he was, and by
whom he is also celebrated among the nobles of Campania in that poem
entitled Gerusalema Conqista, *Book 20:*

> *Fra cavalier magnanimi e cortesi*
> *Risplende il Manso.*[1]

Manso honored the present author during his stay in Naples with the great-
est kindness, and did him many acts of courtesy. Therefore, that he might
not seem ungrateful, his guest, before he left the city, sent him this poem.

These verses also the Muses intend for your praise,
Manso, already well known to Phoebus Apollo's choir,
who has been deemed worthy of honor equal to that
which Gallus once enjoyed and Etruscan Maecenas.[2]
If the breath of my Muse permits me, you too shall sit among
those who wear the victor's crown of ivy and laurel.
A happy friendship once united you with Tasso,
who inscribed your name on his everlasting pages. Later,
the knowing Muse recommended you to sweet Marino[3]
who was proud to call you his foster son while he sang his long   10
tale of the loves of the gods and lulled the nymphs of Rome
into a pleasant drowse. And when he died he left you
his bones to bury (as well as the cost of erecting his tomb).

---

1. Among the magnanimous and courteous cavaliers / Manso shines.

2. Gallus was Virgil's friend and the subject of his Eclogue X. Maecenas was patron to Virgil
and other Augustan poets.

3. Giambattista Marino (also Giovan Battista Marino, 18 October 1569–25 March 1625), born
in Naples, is most famous for his very long epic *L'Adone*.

Your piety and love both show themselves in the bronze
memorializing him, for we see in his smiling visage
his friendly gratitude. But your dedication shows
itself in other ways as well for both of these poets.
You wished to snatch them both from Orcus undiminished
and as far as you could to cheat the laws of the greedy Fates.
You have written down the accounts of their ancestry, their lives   20
harassed by varying fortunes, their characters and their gifts
of talent from Minerva. In this you were emulating
Herodotus who recounted the life of Aeolian Homer.
Therefore, dear Manso, in the name of the Muse Clio
and mighty Pheobus Apollo, I, who have come from the north,
wish you excellent health and a life that will be long-lasting.
I rely upon your kindness not to dismiss a foreign
Muse who, meagerly nourished under the frozen Bear,
has ventured to come south to visit Italian cities.
But even along the banks of our silvery Thames I have heard   30
through the dark hours of night the graceful swans singing.
Indeed, we have even had Tityrus[4] here on these shores.

  We live through the long nights of protracted winter seasons
and look up to see Boötes which is not far from the Plough,
but we are not on that account utterly untaught
and useless to Apollo. Our ancient native Druids
worshipped him and, until age came upon them, sent him
ears of corn, baskets of rosy apples, flowers,
and troops of maidens chosen for honor by the priests.
These Druids were skilled in all the rites that delighted the gods   40
and they were accustomed to sing of the deeds of ancient heroes.
They circled their altars chanting, differing hardly at all
from the customs of Greek maidens on the grassy meadows of Delos,

---

4. Tityrus is a conventional pastoral name and appears in Virgil's *Eclogues*. The wit of Milton's
reference comes from the fact that Spenser applied the name to Chaucer.

together singing their praises of Upis, Loxo, and Arge,[5]
who came with their bare beasts stained a cerulean blue
with woad from far off Britain to the twin gods' sanctuary.

Therefore, lucky old man,[6] wherever Torquato's glory
and name shall be mentioned with reverence throughout the civilized
  world,
wherever the fame of Marino endures and is passed on,
your name and fame as well shall be on the lips of men,   50
and as those two poets fly through the sky forever
you shall be up there between them, no doubt enjoying the view,
for Apollo dwelt in your house with the Muses as his handmaids.
It was not of his own free will that the god came down from heaven
to serve for a time as a shepherd in the household of Admetus.[7]
When he wanted to avoid the noisy herdsmen and farmers
he went to a well-known cave of Chiron not far from the River
Peneus, and there he sang to the sound of a cithern
beneath an ilex to lighten the burdens of labor and exile.
Neither the riverbanks nor the rocks in the lowest chasms   60
stood fixed in their places, but danced to the heavenly music.
Mount Oeta became giddy and shrugged off the weight of its forests.
The ash trees uprooted themselves and wandered about the hillsides,
and the spotted lynxes were soothed and sat on their haunches to listen.

Loved by the gods as you are, Jupiter must have been friendly
even at your birth. Phoebus, the god of arts,
and Hermes, who discovered harmony and invented
the lyre, must have poured their light and grace upon you.
How else can one explain your friendship with great poets?

5. Herodotus mentions Upis and Arge as Hyperborean nymphs who came to Delos as British
Druids to offer gifts to Apollo and Artemis; Loxo is another nymph, an invention of Callimachus.

6. This is an echo of a line from Virgil's Eclogue I that also begins, "Fortunate senex!
ergo . . . "

7. Apollo had incurred the anger of Zeus by killing the Cyclopes. Zeus would have killed
him, but Latona, Apollo's mother, intervened, and he reduced the sentence to a year in servitude.
Apollo then served as a shepherd for Admetus.

Your old age is decked with many lingering flowers   70
and you are yet full of life, the yarn on the spindles of fate
still strong so that your brow retains all of its honors
and your mind has kept the keenness it had back in its prime.
If I ever remember in song the days of our ancient kings
when Arthur set wars in motion even beneath the earth;
if ever I describe the actions of our great heroes
who were brothers around his table; and, if the spirit permits me,
tell of the fight of the Britons against the Saxon hordes,
then may the gods grant me such a great friend as you,
one who knows well the honor due to the sons of Phoebus.   80
When I have completed the span of life the Fates have allotted,
and if I have not been mute for much of that time, this friend
as full of years as tears will give my ashes their due,
and as he stood there in mourning, my spirit would say to him:
"Let me be under your care." He would make sure that my limbs,
relaxed in ashy death, were gathered gently together
and put in a well-wrought urn. It might also happen that he
would have my features reproduced in snowy marble,
my stone locks decked with a garland also of stone
but representing in marble branches of Cyprian myrtle   90
and the laurel boughs of Parnassus. I should then rest easy.
If there be any justice that operates in the world
and if righteousness is rewarded in the way that it deserves,
I, removed to the high ethereal realm of the gods,
to which hard work and courage and a pure mind ought to expect
admission, I shall look down to see these deeds of yours
from whatever part of the secret world the Fates have assigned me,
and, with my mind serene, my face wreathed in smiles,
and suffused with light, I shall clap my hands in thanks and praise.

Damon's Epitaph

Thyrsis and Damon, shepherds of the same neighborhood and following the same pursuits, were most intimate friends from boyhood. Thyrsis, who had gone abroad to improve his mind, received news of Damon's death. After he returns home to find that the news is true, he deplores himself and his solitude in this poem. Under the guise of Damon is here understood Charles Diodati, connected on his father's side with the Tuscan city of Lucca, otherwise an Englishman, a youth who, while he lived, was distinguished for his genius, learning, and other notable virtues.

You nymphs of the River Himera,[1] remembering Daphnis and Hylas,
and the sad fate of Bion,[2] sing your Sicilian dirge
through the cities along the Thames. Tell what murmurs of grief
Thyrsis poured forth and with what unending complaint
he filled the caves, the rivers, the eddying fountains, the deep
groves while he mourned for his friend Damon, snatched away,
and wandered lamenting in lonely places long into the night.
Twice the green stalks had risen and ripened in farmers' fields
and twice had the harvesters come to gather the golden ears
since Damon had been borne down to the land of shades,   10
and Thyrsis had not been there! Love of the Muse had kept him
in a distant Tuscan city. But when he had filled his mind
and his obligations called him home again, he sat
once more beneath his accustomed elm tree and he felt
the fresh truth of the loss, and thus he began to vent
to the ears of the woods and streams and fields his measureless
   sorrow:

1. A river in Sicily thought to have been the "bucolic" stream of Theocritus, who was the father of pastoral poetry.
2. Daphnis was the shepherd (in Theocritus and Ovid) whom a nymph changed to stone. Hylas and Bion are conventional names of pastoral characters, perhaps meant to refer to friends of Milton and Diodati.

"Go home, unfed, my lambs.[3] Your master is occupied
and cannot feed you now. What deities shall I invoke
now that you have been torn away by greedy death?
How can you leave me this way? And can your virtues go   20
without a name to be merged with the other obscure shades?
Let Mercury with the golden wand who marshals the dead,
recognizing your merits, lead you to a select
group that is worthy of you and keep the base herd away.
     "Go home unfed, my lambs. Your master is occupied
and cannot feed you now. Be assured, my friend,
that, unless the wolf comes upon me,[4] you shall not molder away
in your tomb unwept and unmourned. Your honor shall still live
and flourish among the shepherds. Second only to Daphnis[5]
shall they do their duty to you and speak of you with praise   30
for as long as Pales and Faunus love the meadows and fields
and the ancient faith endures, and as long as Minerva's arts
shall continue to inspire mankind to poems and music.
     "Go home unfed, my lambs. Your master is occupied
and cannot feed you now. Remember Damon, rewards
you earned in life are certain and shall be always yours.
I am the one who is the more aggrieved, for where
shall I find a faithful friend such as you to be at my side
through bitter cold and places in which the rough winds blow
or under the blazing sun where the plants have been baked brown? 40
Who will go with me as you did into dangerous country
where lions are within a spear's throw or wolves lurk

3. The unfed sheep are conventional in pastoral poetry as a way of showing the shepherd's grief.
     4. The belief was that any man who met a wolf and did not catch its eye would be struck mute.
     5. Daphnis was the son of Hermes and a Sicilian nymph, so handsome that both Pan and Apollo loved him. He fell in love with Nomia, a river nymph, and she yielded herself to him, but with the warning that if he was ever unfaithful to her, she would strike him blind. He was, she did, and the songs he sang thereafter were of even greater beauty.

waiting for their chance to attack the sheep in the fold?
Who will ease my day with excellent talk and song?
  "Go home unfed, my lambs. Your master is occupied
and cannot feed you now. In whom can I confide?
Who will soothe my troubled mind and get me through
the long dark night with pleasant conversation?
I remember how we roasted pears in the hearth together
as the fire crackled in which we toasted nuts—outside   50
the south wind had brought in a storm that raged in turmoil
and tousled the upper branches of stately and dignified elms.
  "Go home unfed, my lambs. Your master is occupied
and cannot feed you now. When the earth spins on its axle
to bring on summer's heat and Pan seeks out the shade
in a grove of oaks, when the nymphs return to their usual lairs
beside and beneath the flowing waters of the streams they love,
when the plowman takes his ease and dozes under some hedge,
who will bring me distractions, your laughter, and Attic wit,
your learning, culture, and charm I loved and came to rely on?   60
  "Go home unfed, my lambs. Your master is occupied
and cannot feed you now. I wander the fields alone
and walk through the pastures without your company. In the shade
of boughs down in the valley, I wait as evening comes on
and I hear the rain overhead in the canopy of tree leaves.
The southeast wind sighs as if it shared my sadness
and the dusk of the forest is broken with feeble gleams of light.
  "Go home unfed, my lambs. Your master is occupied
and cannot feed you now. My fields that once were tilled
are choked with weeds and the tall corn is drooping with blight.   70
The grapes in the vineyard wither and fall away from the stake.
The myrtle trees don't charm me. The sheep are a bore: they turn
their baleful faces toward their master in silent reproach.
  "Go home unfed, my lambs. Your master is occupied
and cannot feed you now. Tityrus calls to the hazel,

as Alphesiboeus does to the ash, and Aegon to willows,
while fair Amyntas[6] addresses the flowing waters of rivers:
　" 'Here are cool fountains,' they tell me, 'and mossy dells.
Here are the zephyrs, and here the arbutus whispers and soothes
along the banks of attractive and peaceful brooks and streams.' 　　80
But deaf to their songs, I venture deeper into the thickets.
　"Go home unfed, my lambs, your master is occupied
and cannot feed you now. Then Mopsus spoke up, a friend
who had noted my return and was well versed in the stars'
courses in the heavens and the various birdsongs:
　" 'What is this, Thyrsis? What bile disturbs your balance of
　　　humors?
Are you wasting away in love? Or does some unfortunate star
cast its spell upon you? Saturn is often hostile
to shepherds. Have his slanting shafts pierced your breast?'
　"Go home unfed, my lambs. Your master is occupied 　　　　90
and cannot feed you now. The nymphs are amazed and cry:
　" 'What will become of you, Thyrsis? What is it that you want?
The brow of a young man ought not to be furrowed or cloudy,
the eyes should not be stern or the visage austere. A youth
should sing and dance and play at sports and fall in love.
Love that comes too late is more often bitter than sweet.'
　"Go home unfed, my lambs. Your master is occupied
and cannot feed you now. Hyas and Dryope came
and Aegle as well, the daughter of Baucis, skilled at the lyre
but rather proud. And Chloris appeared, a river nymph. 　　　100
Their comforting words did not have any effect whatever,
for nothing can cheer or move me now, or ever will.
　"Go home unfed, my lambs. Your master is occupied
and cannot feed you now. I look at a herd of cattle
that wander about the meadow and see how alike they are,

6. These are more conventional pastoral names, presumably representing friends of the poet.

each a companion to all. None seeks out from among them
a special friend. And jackals in the same way come in packs
to feed on whatever they can. And shaggy wild asses roam
together. So it is on the shore where the seal and walrus
calves troop together. The sparrows that fly in the air   110
soar and wheel together, each one having a mate,
and then at the end of the day they all return to their nests—
but if through some evil chance a kite or sparrow hawk
should strike one of them dead or a bumpkin on the ground
bring one down with his arrow, the bird that is bereft
will seek at once a new mate to be his partner in flight.
But men are a stony breed, vexed by the hostile fates
and alien one from another in discordant minds and hearts.
From among hundreds and thousands, hardly can one find
a kindred spirit. And if through good fortune one does   120
encounter such an answer to his hopes and prayers, in a moment
that friend is snatched away, leaving a wound of grief.

"Go home unfed, my lambs. Your master is occupied
and cannot feed you now. What could I have been thinking,
wanting to leave behind our snowy cliffs and cross
the Alps to see what was left of ancient Rome and improve
my mind and taste? Even if it were still the same
as when Tityrus[7] left his flocks behind to see it,
how could I have parted from such a boon companion
and put between us so many seas, mountains, rocks,   130
roaring streams, and forests? Had I been less ambitious
and stayed behind I might have touched his hand at the last
and even closed the eyes of him who was peacefully dying.
I might have said, 'Farewell, remember me, my friend,
when you take your rightful place among the stars in heaven.'

"Go home unfed, my lambs. Your master is occupied

---

7. In Virgil's first Eclogue, Meliboeus asks Tityrus what Rome was like?

and cannot feed you now. I shall never weary of thinking
of my Tuscan shepherd friends, young men who loved the Muses
but here too were grace and charm. You too, Damon, could claim
Tuscany in your line, which came from ancient Lucca.   140
How happy I was to lie by the banks of the murmuring Arno,
stretched out in the poplar groves on the softest grass, and perhaps
plucking violets or sprays of myrtle while I listened
to Menalcas contend with Lycidas in the art of singing sweetly.
I even dared to join in the competition and did
not too badly, I think, for I still have with me those gifts
with which you presented me—reed baskets, earthenware bowls,
and shepherds' pipes. Both Dati and Francini,[8] who were renowned
for eloquence and learning, and both of Lydian blood,[9]
have inscribed my name in the bark of beech trees in their groves.   150
    "Go home unfed, my lambs. Your master is occupied
and cannot feed you now. In my lunatic delusion
when I was happily shutting my kids in their wattled pen,
I would talk to myself and say, when you were already dead:
'Now Damon is singing, or stretching nets to catch the hares.
Now he is plaiting reeds for baskets and other such uses.'
What I hoped for the future, I seized upon and imagined
as also going on in the present progressive tense.
    "Ah, good friend, does some obligation call upon you,
or can we go down to lie in the murmuring shade by the Colne[10]   160
and chat together? Or somewhere else in the countryside?
You can show me the various healing herbs and juices,
the hellebore, the crocus, the hyacinth leaf, and whatever
other plants the marshes offer and you can explain

    8. Dati and Francini, two of the "Tuscan shepherds," are Carlo Dati and Antonio Francini,
both of whose work Milton had praised.
    9. According to Herodotus, the Lydians migrated to northern Italy after a famine and be-
came the Etruscans and Tuscans.
    10. The river dividing Middlesex and Buckinghamshire. It flows near Horton, where Milton
lived for some years.

their uses in the healing arts that you know so well.

"But to hell with the herbs and simples! To hell with the doctor's
    arts!

What good have they done their master? How have they profited me?

It is now eleven nights and a day, and I put my lips

to the pipes but they broke apart, for they could not sustain

the deep tones I attempted. Nevertheless I will tell   170

my tale. You forests, now be still and pay attention.

"Go home unfed, my lambs. Your master is occupied

and cannot feed you now. I would tell of the Trojan ships

off the shores of Camden in the realm of Imogen.[11]

I will sing of Belinus and Brennus[12] and also of Arviragus,[13]

as well as Constantine's settlement of Britons in western Gaul

under British laws. I will sing of pregnant Igraine[14]

to whom Uther appeared with the face and arms of Gorlois.

Then, if life remains, I shall hang my pipe on a pine

far away and forgotten, unless it forsakes the old   180

Arcadian songs to sound, instead, a British theme.

And why not, after all? One man cannot undertake

all things. My rewards shall be more than ample if I—

altogether unknown in foreign parts—shall be read

along the River Ouse[15] by those who drink the waters

of the Alaun,[16] the eddying Abra,[17] the Trent, and the River Thames.

---

11. According to Geoffrey of Monmouth, Pandrassus was a king of Greece, defeated by Brutus, to whom he then gave his daughter Imogen. Brutus' realm in Britain is therefore called the realm of Imogen.

12. Brenus and Belinus marched victoriously through Gaul and took part in the sack of Rome in 390 BCE.

13. Arviragus was the son of King Cymbeline. After Cymbeline's death, Julius Caesar invaded Britain, and later Arviragus submitted to Claudius Caesar, whose daughter Genuissa he married.

14. Igraine, or Iogern, was the wife of King Gorlois of Cornwall. After his death, Uther Pendragon, with the help of Merlin, appeared to her in the shape of her dead husband and begat Arthur, the heroic king.

15. A river that rises in Oxfordshire and flows into the Wash.

16. Either the combined mouths of the Stour and the Avon, which Ptolemy called the Alaun, or perhaps the Alne, in Northumberland.

17. The Humber

By the quickly flowing Tamar[18] and the shores of the distant
    Orkneys
I shall hope to find my congenial and friendly readers.
    "Go home unfed, my lambs. Your master is occupied
and cannot feed you now. These are the things I was keeping   190
under the bark of the laurel to bring them to you later,
these and more besides. I wanted also to show you
a matched pair of handsome cups that Manso gave me,
treasures really, with double bands of carving on them
around the base. Then, higher up is the Red Sea
and oases in which one can all but smell the frankincense
on the far-off coast of Arabia where, in the balsam groves
the bright blue phoenix flies, with its wings of many colors,
that nonpareil on earth. It watches Aurora rise
over the glassy waves of the slowly brightening sea.   200
Higher yet, around the rim, there are scenes of Olympus
and the whole expanse of heaven. Who would believe such a thing?
But there's still more, for here is Love with his little quiver,
his flashing arms, his torch, and his darts that are tipped in bronze,
all of them depicted within a suggested cloud
from which he takes his aim—not at the ignoble
hearts and souls of the rabble, but only at worthy targets.
He rolls his flashing eyes this way and that in search
of suitable subjects, and therefore, choosing the noblest minds
and most nearly perfect faces and figures, he shoots and inflames   210
only those whom he deems the best and the most worthy.
    "You are among these Damon. Surely my friendship and hope
do not deceive me. You must be among these chosen,
for where should your sweet simplicity go and where
should your spotless virtue find its right and appropriate home?
It would be a mistake to seek you in Lethean Orcus.

18. A river between Cornwall and Devonshire

Tears do not become you, and therefore I'll weep no more.
No more tears for Damon who dwells in the highest heaven,
which is what his life deserved. He has walked on the rainbow
and among the blessed in heaven and the everlasting gods   220
he drinks the celestial waters of joy with his pious lips.
Having a station in heaven with the rights of such a place,
stand by my side, watch over, protect, and defend your friend,
whatever your name be now—Damon, or Diodati,
which is how the others in heaven will probably know and address
      you.
Here in the groves of the forest, we shall still call you Damon.
You were a youth who had never tasted the pleasures of marriage,
and thus for you are reserved the honors due to a virgin.
Your noble head will be bound by a coronet and your hands
will bear the pilgrim's palm while you reenact forever   230
the nuptial rites of immortals, as songs and lyre music
combine with angelic dances, rapturous and joyful,
in the revels in which the thyrsus[19] of Zion forever reigns.

19. The thyrsus is a staff entwined with vines and ivy that was borne by the Bacchantes, but here it is Christianized to become a heavenly symbol.

To John Rouse, Librarian of Oxford University
January 23, 1646

On a lost volume of my poems which he asked me to send him a second time that he might place it with my other works in the public library.

STROPHE I

Twofold book, got up in a single dress
and yet with double pages,[1]
bright with the panache a youth's hand
chose to lavish upon it—
a mere beginner's work—
some that the author wrote in Ausonian[2] shades,
and also some in the pleasant British landscape,
but ignoring the turmoil of his countrymen,[3]
he did this work with an Italian quill,
giving himself to their native instruments,   10
and wrote in the hope of pleasing those who were then around him,
essaying a foreign strain
with his feet not quite touching solid ground.

ANTISTROPHE

Little book who surreptitiously left
your brothers when, at my friend's request,
you started on your illustrious journey
from the city of London on to the Thames.[4]
There are the Muses' fountains
and there the Bacchantes dance
as all the world knows.   20

---

1. The volume was a double book bound as one, the first with English poems and the second with Latin, with separate pagination and title pages.
2. Italian.
3. The struggles between king and Parliament, Anglicans and Puritans.
4. The Isis, Oxford's river, and the Thames are continuous.

It will be famous forever
as long as the heavens revolve
in their appointed orbits and courses
throughout the endless passage of time.
Those were the objects of my thought.

STROPHE 2
What merciful god or demigod,
taking pity on the genius of our nation—
if we have atoned enough for our earlier faults
and have thrown off unmanly sloth—
will end at last this accursed strife   30
among our suffering citizens?
What divinity will return us
to pious and nurturing study and summon the Muses back
who have been driven out
from almost all of England?[5]
Who will rid us of all these Harpies
and drive Phineus'[6] pests far away from our river.

ANTISTROPHE
But poor little book, stolen or just lost,
you have somehow wandered off somewhere
and instead of joining your brothers have gone   40
to some dark den or hiding place
that now confines you where some dirty calloused hand
paws you and possibly rubs your delicate binding,
not having the faintest idea who you are.
Nevertheless, be happy and even rejoice,

---

5. The Civil War had broken out in 1642, and Oxford was the Royalist headquarters. With
much of the university transformed into a garrison, ordinary academic activities were suspended.

6. Phineus, king of Thrace, was plagued by Harpies that snatched away his food and fouled
it with their excrement. He was delivered from this torment by the Argonauts.

for you may escape from Lethe's depths
and soar to reach Jupiter's courts.

STROPHE 3
Rejoice for Rouse to whom
you have been sent and from whom you may expect
the care he gives to the very finest   50
monuments of all mankind. For you to be
among his treasures is gratifying indeed.
He asked that you be sent to him,
to fulfill a promise I made and to fill a gap
in his library's extensive holdings.
You will take a proud place
in the sacred inner chamber
where he himself presides,
the faithful guardian of all our immortal treasures,
worth more than the golden tripods   60
Ion[7] held at ancient Delphi.

ANTISTROPHE
Therefore you shall go to the pleasant
groves where the Muses dwell,
the divine abode of Phoebus Apollo where
he has settled himself in the vale of Oxford.
He prefers it now to Delos
and the twin peaks of Parnassus.
An honor to go there,
and a greater honor for you to have been invited
by my so propitious, so discerning friend.   70
There you shall take our place among the best

7. Ion was son of Apollo and Creusa and was the guardian of his father's treasures at the temple at Delphi.

authors who have been the bright lights
and the glory of the Greek and Roman peoples.

EPODE
You are what my poor talents have managed to bring
forth into the world, and not in vain.
I bid you now a happy, secure rest
beyond the reach of anybody's envy,
a book's ideal home
in the care of Hermes and watchful Rouse
where the course tongue of the vulgar shall never manage to enter   80
and from which any uncouth readers
shall always be far off.
But perhaps remote descendants
in a better age when wiser and purer hearts
will render fairer judgments
and envy is dead in its tomb
posterity will know what my merit is,
thanks to John Rouse.